ASIAN AMERICANS
OF ACHIEVEMENT

APOLO ANTON OHNO

ASIAN AMERICANS
OF ACHIEVEMENT

ASIAN AMERICANS
OF ACHIEVEMENT

APOLO ANTON OHNO

REBECCA ALDRIDGE

CHELSEA HOUSE
PUBLISHERS
An imprint of Infobase Publishing

Apolo Anton Ohno

Copyright © 2009 by Infobase Publishing

Chelsea House
An imprint of Infobase Publishing
132 West 31st Street
New York NY 10001

Library of Congress Cataloging-in-Publication Data
Aldridge, Rebecca.
  Apolo Anton Ohno / by Rebecca Aldridge.
    p. cm. — (Asian Americans of achievement)
  Includes bibliographical references and index.
  ISBN 978-1-60413-565-7 (hardcover : alk. paper) 1. Ohno, Apolo Anton—Juvenile literature. 2. Speed skaters—United States—Biography—Juvenile literature. I. Title.
II. Series.
  GV850.O45A76 2009
  796.91092—dc22
  [B]   2009009918

Series design by Erika K. Arroyo
Cover design by Ben Peterson and Alicia Post
Composition by EJB Publishing Services, Inc.
Cover printed by Yurchak Printing, Landisville, PA
Book printed and bound by Yurchak Printing, Landisville, PA
Date printed: Octobert, 2011
Printed in the United States of America

10 9 8 7 6 5 4 3

This book is printed on acid-free paper.

CONTENTS

An Unstoppable Skater

He positioned himself on the starting line and began to focus. For him, focus is key during any competition. All around him he could hear the roar of the thousands of spectators in the stands, and he knew millions upon millions more were watching from home. Apolo Anton Ohno had fought hard to get here, to the 2002 Winter Olympic Games in Salt Lake City, Utah. His journey thus far had seen him run away from home, almost turn away from the sport he loved, make some hard but crucial decisions, and eventually learn the important lesson of standing up for himself. Four years earlier, he had made it all the way to the U.S. Olympic Trials, only to fail. In these Olympics, expectations for this charismatic 19-year-old short-track skater from Seattle were high. In the NBC commentators' box sat his father, Yuki, his partner in short track, the person who had supported him all along the way.

The gun went off, and the racers shot off the line. The race was the 1,000 meters, and the five skaters had 8¾ laps around the 111-meter oval to fight it out for gold. With only one lap to go, Ohno was in the lead. In short track, though, no one is safe for long, and the other skaters' moves can be unpredictable. Vying for that glory of gold, Li Jiajun of China took his chances, and when he saw a small opening on the outside, he darted ahead, hoping to pass Ohno. Just as quickly as Li made his move, Ohno made a defensive move of his own. In mere seconds, Li was on his way down, but he was not going alone. Ahn Hyun-Soo of South Korea got caught in the Chinese short tracker's downward spill, and almost unbelievably, Canadian skater Mathieu Turcotte found he was out of control and going down as well. Ohno did not remain unscathed. Turcotte's fall caught Ohno and sent him reeling into the boards. His own skate slammed into his inner left thigh, cutting through his skinsuit and creating a gash. With four men down on the ice, one had to ask: Was this short-track speed skating or a demolition derby?

Australian skater Steven Bradbury, who had been at the back of the pack for the duration of the race, sailed past the crumpled skaters to capture the gold. But Ohno was not going to let the race end that easily. Mustering all the strength he had, he began to crawl across the ice. With his leg dripping blood, Ohno sent the crowd into a frenzy as he maneuvered awkwardly across the line to capture the silver medal. It may not have been the most graceful performance, but short track is not always about grace; it is more about speed, strategy, and staying alive in the game. With his limping but determined move, Ohno had done it: He had won his first Olympic medal. It was the first of several to come.

With his good looks, charm, and trademark style—his famous headband and soul patch—not to mention his talent, Ohno became an instant celebrity. Later that year, he was featured as one of *People* magazine's 50 Most Beautiful People. In the magazine, fellow Asian American and Olympic medalist

After a four-skater pileup, Apolo Anton Ohno *(foreground)* crawled toward the finish line during the 1,000-meter short-track speed-skating race at the 2002 Winter Olympics. Ohno was able to finish second, giving him his first Olympic medal. Also struggling to complete the race was Mathieu Turcotte of Canada *(No. 319)*.

Michelle Kwan said of him, "He has everything a guy represents, strength and power." And that was true, but Ohno also had another quality that had helped bring him to the top of his sport: dedication.

Since his start in short-track speed skating in 1995, Ohno had not always taken his sport completely seriously. Such an attitude is easy to understand: He was a teenager, and competing at the international level required a lot of sacrifice. But once Ohno made the decision that short track was what he wanted for his life, he gave it body and soul. He believes that the sacrifices he has made over the years have been worth it because, to him, short track is like nothing else in the world. Ohno has said, "Speed skating is like floating on the ice. When I'm in a great mood and my spirits are light, it's a beautiful feeling." Ohno's valiant Olympic effort in front of millions proved his belief that, if you set your mind to something and give not just 100 percent but 110 percent, anything in life is possible.

2

A Skater Is Born

At the age of 18, a young man named Yuki Ohno made an important and daring decision when he chose to emigrate alone from his home in Tokyo, Japan, to the United States. Yuki's journey brought him to the city of Seattle, Washington, with its cloudy skies and scenic mountains. There, he began to study accounting at Seattle City College, but the young man from Japan, who had come from a family that believed strongly in education (his father was the vice president of a Japanese university), soon discovered that accounting was not for him. He liked people. He enjoyed the buzz of conversation and the lively atmosphere of being social. He could not picture himself behind a desk, sitting all day with nothing but numbers staring him in the face. So, Yuki left the college and moved toward a completely different vocation, cosmetology.

The art of hairstyling appealed to the former accounting student, and the lifestyle of a hairdresser suited Yuki completely. Part of his studies included time at the famous Vidal

(continues on page 14)

Story of My Family

A FATHER'S UNORTHODOX PATH

Apolo Anton Ohno's father took many risks as a young man—like leaving Japan and pursuing cosmetology. In an excerpt from *A Journey: The Autobiography of Apolo Anton Ohno*, Apolo tells of his father's childhood and subsequent move to the United States:

My dad was born in Tokyo, Japan. His father was a state university vice president. From kindergarten on, he was on the educational fast track there, which is like aiming for an Ivy League school, but more competitive because there are fewer colleges to choose from. In Japan parents push their kids so hard in school because it promises job security and safety.

Dad's early life was spent studying and every year he had to take tests in order to achieve the next level in school. It's not like the U.S., where you hear of kids getting passed to the next grade before they can read or write. If you don't pass the tests in Japan, you don't move on and that puts you on a different, less prestigious, and lower-income career path. Pretty much, one mess-up and it's over.

In high school Dad slept five hours a night and spent his waking hours cramming, memorizing, and practicing for exams. He did what his parents expected of him and never questioned the hard work or his own desires. He progressed every year, but there was never time to enjoy his success because each year involved another enormous test. One day in high school he looked around his classroom and noticed that everyone's expression was the same—just a mask of concentration, because they were all working toward a university education and there was a lot of pressure. My dad decided he didn't want to be there anymore.

At age eighteen, and speaking only rudimentary English, my father came to the United States. He'd wanted to visit for some time, but had no idea that he was going to stay. He ended up in Portland, Oregon. His parents were very disappointed when he didn't come home, but Dad was young, happy, and had very few responsibilities. He worked as a janitor, waiter, newspaper deliveryman, bartender, you name it, and then decided he wanted to travel to Seattle. The problem was, he pronounced it "Sheetle," and nobody understood when he asked for directions. He always jokes that one of the greatest things about Americans is their willingness to try to figure out what a foreigner is saying. In Europe, if they don't understand you, they slam the door. Eventually Dad found his way to Seattle.

Somehow, between looking for new jobs, my dad ended up in beauty school. He won a contest within the first year. He'd spent so long struggling to figure out what he wanted to do with his life, and it suddenly became clear. My father has an artistic personality and he'd found his outlet. In the early seventies Dad traveled to London, which at the time was packed with artists. Hairdressing there was a higher skill, and he studied at the Vidal Sassoon school at the height of its popularity. There he learned the precision cut—haircutting that doesn't depend upon curlers or dryers but upon the cut itself to make the shape. At the time it was a revolutionary idea. He had tons of friends, visited salons to watch stylists work, and studied haircutting like it was sculpture. The lifestyle was nonstop, and my dad had a blast.

By the time he returned to Seattle, my father was in demand and did a lot of teaching and training in addition to his own work as a stylist. He was a workaholic, applying in his new profession his ability to study long hours. The powerful difference now was that he loved his job and was driven to succeed.

(continued from page 11)

Sassoon salon in London, and early in his career, he worked as a stylist in New York for some of the top fashion models. He enjoyed the company of other young beauty professionals like himself, often hanging out and partying. He also partied with the people he met in the fashion industry, as well as artists. Yuki says that his wild side was showing, a side he would come to see years later in his only son.

Eventually, Yuki increased his responsibilities by becoming a business owner and opening his own salon in Seattle in 1980, Yuki's Diffusions. As a small-business owner, he had to cut down on the traveling he once enjoyed, but he still liked late nights of partying and entertaining with friends. Occasionally, he would get a taste of his previous lifestyle and fly off to London to do the hair of a beautiful model.

THE STYLIST BECOMES A FATHER

In the early 1980s, at the age of 36, Yuki met and married an 18-year-old woman named Jerrie Lee, and on May 22, 1982, the two experienced the birth of a child, a precious baby boy whom they named Apolo Anton. The birth of Apolo would change Yuki's life forever. The hardworking hairdresser soon became a single father, after Jerrie Lee abruptly left her husband and infant son before his first birthday, never to see Apolo again.

Because Yuki had taken that long journey from Tokyo to Seattle, he had no family support to help him raise a young child—every care, every need for his son would be his to deal with alone. Yuki's days of partying were over; in their place were long days of working to support himself and the son he dearly loved. Gone were the luxuries of buying and dressing in the latest fashions and stepping out in the shine of carefully polished shoes. Life for Yuki had become a little less recognizable.

As a stylist who often worked evening hours and Saturdays, Yuki did not have an easy time finding child care. And what did he know about day care, he wondered. For that matter, what did he know about raising a child? But he was a father now, and Yuki took his responsibility seriously. Each morning, he would drive his son to day care, put in a 12-hour day, and then pick Apolo up later than most of the other children—around 7 or 8 in the evening. Yuki felt a bit out of place when dropping off or picking up Apolo at day care; all of the other children had mothers who seemed to know so much more than he did. They brought little comforts for their sons and daughters, like blankets or stuffed animals to give them a little reassurance while away from home; Yuki had not thought to do the same. The new father, though, paid attention. He watched, observed, and learned—again a trait he would see when his son took up the sport of speed skating.

The struggle was worth it for Yuki. He loved his son completely and would try to spend as much time with him as he could, which was not easy with his grueling schedule. Whenever he had a weekend that was not filled with clients, Yuki would savor that time with his child.

THE IMPISH LITTLE APOLO

In day care, tiny Apolo began to demonstrate his talent for the physical, as well as his devilish side. He was known for jumping the fence and for climbing all the way to the top of the playground's jungle gym and then refusing to come down. From time to time, the other children would dare Apolo to do things like eat dirt and rocks, and fearless Apolo would kindly oblige. But these were not the only aspects of Apolo's personality that became apparent early on. By the time Apolo was three, his father was convinced that he was gifted because he picked up on things so quickly. Later, when Apolo was in school, Yuki discovered at a parent-teacher conference that his boy was not paying attention in class—he had ignored a French lesson and instead started to read a book. Yuki assumed Apolo was simply

Apolo Anton Ohno and his father, Yuki, celebrated in Seattle, Washington, after the 2002 Winter Olympic Games. Apolo was not even a year old when his mother left the family and Yuki Ohno became a single father. Yuki channeled Apolo's youthful energy into many activities, from singing in a choir to competitive swimming and roller-skating.

bored, which prompted him to find a different school for his bright, but unfocused, son.

Another outlet Yuki tried as a way to focus young Apolo's beaming energy was swimming classes. He enrolled Apolo at age 6 in a small program that had young swimmers of varying levels. In the program, each participant had to work his or her way through six levels before making it to the competition stage. The fun-loving Apolo, however, goofed around more than he swam. Apolo's behavior did not deter Yuki. Convinced that swimming was still the right avenue, but that the program had the wrong structure, Yuki paid to place his son in a private swimmers' club. The participants there were quite serious about their sport, and most went six days a week. In contrast, Apolo was only able to attend three days a week, but in this different atmosphere, Apolo found a new feeling in his gut, a desire to win. This new sense of competition gave Apolo a drive he had not had before, and he was able to keep up with kids who were practicing twice as much as he was.

Yuki found other activities to channel his son's abundant energy. Apolo, though, did not necessarily enjoy every activity. One that he did like was roller-skating, especially on those infamous rainy Seattle days. His father had gotten him involved at age 7 and took him every Thursday after school. But singing in the Northwest Boys Choir (Apolo had a three-octave voice before hitting puberty) was another story altogether.

LIFE WITH A SINGLE DAD

By age 8, Apolo was a good student, growing up as a latchkey kid who, by necessity, learned to take care of himself. When the school day ended, he worked on his homework alone, without a parent nearby to field questions or provide help. He prepared his dinner and then got himself off to bed. On days when he did not have schoolwork or sports practice, he preferred being outside riding his bike or playing football to sitting indoors watching television. Although this life may have been a bit lonely, Apolo today has fond memories of his childhood and the special times he and his father were able to share.

During breaks from school, Apolo stayed close to his father and seemed to mimic the social-butterfly lifestyle of the hairdresser's earlier days, hanging out at the back of the salon and chatting with Yuki's clients. The two also liked to get away and spend time in the outdoors hiking and camping.

Apolo especially enjoyed the time he spent with his father at Copalis Beach, a spot 150 miles (241 kilometers) away from the hustle and bustle of Seattle. There, they rented a wood cabin with a porch overlooking the Pacific Ocean. It was a quiet place to spend quality time together walking along the shoreline, breathing in the salty air, watching the seagulls fly with grace overhead, and taking in the beauty of the nearby forests and mountain streams. After a day out in this peaceful setting, Apolo and his father would sit in the cabin and sketch out the experiences that had filled their day. Little did Apolo or his father know at the time, but in later years, this cabin with its memories and its remoteness would play a crucial part in the shaping of an Olympic champion.

WHAT'S IN A NAME?

Many people have the misconception that the champion skater was named after the Olympian god Apollo, but that is not true. Apolo's father explained the origin of his son's name to him during one of their treasured trips to the cabin at Copalis Beach. Yuki had come across the word in a dictionary soon after his son's birth. "Ap" meant to steer away from and "lo," the dictionary explained, was akin to meaning "look out, here he comes." That meaning struck Yuki, which is why he chose it for his son. The young champion's middle name, Anton, means priceless.

Apolo also had a nickname growing up, a nickname that might seem unbelievable now—Chunkie. Apparently, Apolo liked to eat a lot of pizza, and the name reflected his weight. But his whole group of friends went by unusual nicknames. The young swimmer and skater hung out with the likes of Worm, Checkered, Little T, Alpha, Sleepy, and Cupid.

As adolescence approached, Yuki and Apolo's seemingly harmonious relationship became less of one. A rebellious side developed in Apolo. He "blew off" participating in his school's honors program. On weekends, he wanted to spend more time with his friends and less time with his father. And when he could no longer hit the high notes, he gladly left the boys' choir.

Around age 13, Apolo started to associate with a crowd of older boys ranging in age from 16 to 18. Yuki worked hard to keep his son on track, even kicking a couple of the boys out of his house on one occasion because they were skipping swim practice.

MORE THAN A KNACK FOR SPORTS

Apolo had continued with his swimming, and by age 12, he was a state champion in the breaststroke. Yuki took a great deal of pride in his son's accomplishments and had hopes of him someday swimming for the prestigious Stanford University team. The sport, however, did not inspire a feeling of passion in Apolo, even though he had been swimming for a number of years. Doing laps bored him, and he found it tiring. Plus, he had a strong distaste for being submerged in the cold, cold water.

The athlete's sport of preference was skating. Roller-skating on quad skates, those with two wheels in the front and two wheels in the back, was an activity that Apolo did not take too seriously, but he enjoyed it tremendously. What he especially found exhilarating was the speed, and he could not fathom why some kids came to the rink just to play video games in the arcade, when they could be experiencing the excitement of gliding on wheels with the walls of the rink rushing past. Apolo showed prowess in his first competition, a race that took place in Lynwood, Washington. He skated well, taking second place and receiving accolades from his proud father as well as a trophy for his room, but that was not

A group of skaters takes the corner in the 500-meter short-track race at the 1994 Winter Olympics in Lillehammer, Norway. Apolo watched the Olympic short-track races that year with his father and was mesmerized by the speed the skaters attained. Apolo, who had been competing as an inline roller skater, knew he wanted to get out on the ice.

enough for Apolo. Second wasn't first, so to the young skater, second wasn't really a success.

Eventually, Apolo joined a rink in Auburn, Washington, where he participated in his first race wearing inline skates rather than quad skates. Once the race began, he flew past his competitors—all wearing quad skates—and took first place. The victory, though, felt a bit tainted to Apolo. He felt that his skates, not his ability, had won him the race. Apolo's performance, though, had certainly been inspiring, because after that competition all the other kids in the program started to use inline skates, too.

Yuki saw the potential his son had in the sport, as well as the potential for competitive inline skating to keep Apolo out of trouble. So for the next two years, they hopped into their tiny and rusted Volkswagen Rabbit to drive miles and miles to any and every race they could. Apolo's father was devoted to his son's cause. He worked tirelessly all day only to drive through the night to get Apolo to the next competition. Even bad weather did not stop them from their quest. Rain could pour, snow could blow, but the pair would still get in the car and drive. Yuki once drove 20 hours straight to get his son to Missouri—along slick and dangerous roads during a snowstorm, all without the benefit of four-wheel drive. Their tenacity paid off—just as Apolo had earned the title of state champion in the breaststroke, he won the title of national inline skating champion for his age division.

THE CHANGING POINT

In the snowy winter season of 1994, something that could have been just an everyday occurrence made all the difference in Apolo's life. He and his father sat down together to watch the 1994 Winter Olympic Games in Lillehammer, Norway. Apolo's eyes went wide while watching the short-track skating event. He was floored by the speed the skaters reached as they glided around the ice rink. Even Yuki was captivated. That was all Apolo needed, to see those skaters on TV—he wanted to learn to skate just like them. The following Christmas, "Santa" placed a special present under the tree—a new pair of speed skates. Life for Apolo Anton Ohno was about to change—in a big way.

3

The Rebel Skater

So Santa had brought Apolo Anton Ohno his dream gift, but there was still a slight problem. Just because he had the skates did not mean that Apolo knew how to use them. Yuki found a short-track club for Apolo in Eugene, Oregon, five hours away from their home near Seattle. The distance was of no consequence to either of them; they were both committed to giving short-track skating a try.

Of course, Apolo had experience with inline skating, but this was different—blades and ice, instead of wheels and ground. Apolo watched the other skaters and did his best on the ice, but he struggled; he just could not seem to get the hang of how to simply glide on the ice. Apolo was grateful when another skater stopped to give him a kindly hint: He needed to sharpen his blades. The skater told him that new blade edges are serrated. Before hitting the ice, a skater needs to use a sharpener to whittle down those serrated ridges. Once the ridges are gone, gliding becomes much easier. From this exchange, Apolo realized that short-track speed skating was more than just skates and ice. He had a lot of learning ahead of him.

At the club in Eugene, Apolo took part in his first race. Even after sharpening his skate blades as recommended, Apolo found himself outskated three times by a little girl with a bobbing blond ponytail. That first day of competition still held some semblance of victory for the new skater. He patted himself on the back for two reasons: not once falling down and finally finishing ahead of the ponytailed girl in the day's last race.

Apolo eventually left the club in Eugene for one a bit closer to home in Vancouver, British Columbia. In Vancouver, people took the sport of short track more seriously. Here, Apolo was surrounded by a better class of skaters, people he could observe and learn from, people on whom he could model his own skating. He watched these skaters much the same way his

INLINE VS. SHORT TRACK

It did not take long for Apolo Ohno to find out that the worlds of short-track skating and inline skating were very different. For one thing, Apolo was used to the "trash talking" banter between inline-skating competitors. When he first tried to intimidate short-track opponents with trash talk, Apolo was met with blank stares and silence. He learned quickly to keep his mouth shut. Although he had found that kind of talk fun with his inline-skating chums, he also appreciated short-track competitors for not resorting to that behavior.

Making friends did not come easily. The other athletes Apolo skated with knew his background—that he had been an inline skater—and inline skating gave Apolo an endurance advantage that his competitors did not necessarily have. In short track, Apolo says, skaters who come from the inline world are feared and looked down upon.

father had watched the mothers at Apolo's day care to learn about parenting.

Apolo's life was now filled with weekend competitions. At these, his father would record the races with the camera he had once used to videotape his son's swim meets. Then, during the week, Apolo studied the tapes to improve his performance.

APOLO BREAKS OUT

In January 1996, the relatively novice skater took part in the Junior World Championship trials. The 13-year-old was just one face among hundreds of skaters—a nobody. He did not have the name recognition that some of the other skaters had. Still, Apolo could feel the pressure. He was incredibly nervous about exhibiting his new skills in front of so many people. Despite his nerves, Apolo raced his way to a fourth-place overall ranking—not bad for a new guy on the circuit. The performance put him on the map of short-track speed skating.

By the spring of 1996, Apolo was doing remarkably well for himself. He was not only the overall champion for his age division in U.S. Short Track but also for his age division in North American Short Track. He had a group title in U.S. Long Track as well. Yuki realized that his son's quick ascension in the sport could mean something big. He wanted every opportunity for Apolo, so at one competition, Yuki approached Jeroen Otter, then the U.S. senior national head coach. He asked Otter about the next steps for Apolo. Where did they go from here? How could he help get Apolo to the next level in his career?

Otter had no problem discussing the young skater's future. He knew Apolo was good enough for what he was about to suggest. He told Yuki to get Apolo to Lake Placid, New York, and the training program for the U.S. Junior National Development Team. But Apolo's father did not realize that the yearlong residency program had a minimum age requirement of 15. Apolo had only just turned 14. Yuki, though, was undeterred. He took it upon himself to call the head coach of the program, Pat Wentland, directly. What Yuki did not know was that this phone call would soon mean turbulence for the father and son's harmonious relationship.

Apolo's quick progress and remarkable accomplishments persuaded Wentland to go to bat for the teen. The coach convinced the entrance committee that it should let Apolo join as the youngest member ever. There was only one problem— Apolo did not want to go. He was incensed when he heard that

Racing on a 111-meter oval, short-track skaters often have to touch their hands to the ice to maneuver around the tight turns. Apolo Anton Ohno chased Marc Gagnon of Canada during a 3,000-meter qualifying race in 2001 at the World Short Track Speed Skating Team Championships in Japan.

his summer vacation of camping and hanging out with friends would be pre-empted by life in a dorm across the country practicing and training all day. Yuki refused to give up. He would not let his son squander this opportunity.

HITTING TURBULENCE

The Lake Placid program had a June start date, but late into that month, the stubborn skater was still in Washington, where a battle was being fought in the Ohno home. Yuki kept trying to convince his son that the program would do wonders for him. Apolo, though, was strong-willed. He was also scared. Scared of being thousands of miles from his friends and, more important, his father.

THE SPORT OF SHORT-TRACK SPEED SKATING

The history of short-track speed skating is a little cloudy, but what is almost certain is that, in 1906, Canada and the United States held their first competitions in the sport. Long-track skating had been popular in Europe for decades, and most likely, as interest in the sport developed in North America, skaters began to outnumber the available ice tracks. Thus, enthusiastic athletes took to the shorter tracks of hockey rinks and indoor ice rinks as a means of practice. Long-track races are on a 400-meter oval. In short-track skating, the track is 111 meters in length, so what evolved was a sport with shorter straightaways and tighter turns. In fact, the turns are so tight that the skaters actually touch the ice with their hands as they lean far over.

Some view short track as an extreme or contact sport, since the competitors skate only inches from each other at incredible speeds. Unlike long track, in which competitors skate individually against the clock, in short track, four to six competitors skate head-to-head, duking it out on the ice. They may travel at speeds

By the end of the month, Apolo was still resolute about not going, but Yuki's insistence appeared to win out. Against Apolo's wishes, he packed his son's bags and drove him to the airport. The only sound in the car was silence. At the airport, Yuki checked Apolo in, got him his ticket, and walked him down to the departure gate. After wishing his son well, Yuki said goodbye and left. Apolo's father had just made one giant mistake.

Apolo thought quickly. He walked away from the airplane he was set to board and toward a telephone, calling a friend who came and picked him up. The young teen should have been in upstate New York that night; instead he was carousing at a party. The rebel skater did not have much of a plan.

up to 35 miles per hour (56 kilometers per hour), making break-neck turns on sharpened blades only a millimeter wide. In these conditions, bumps and crashes are common, adding to the sport's appeal as well as its danger. Obviously, a short-track skater needs to skate quickly, but he or she also needs to skate with strategy, knowing when and where to pass the competition to make it to the finish line first.

In men's Olympic short track, there are four main events. (In some international competitions, there is also a 3,000-meter individual event.) The shortest of these, requiring a power-ful takeoff, is the 500 meters. The longest individual event is the 1,500 meters, which takes a great deal of endurance on top of strategy to win. The 1,000 meters is a mid-length competition for short-trackers. Finally comes the 5,000-meter team relay featuring four-member teams. Short track is a relatively new Olympic sport. It made its debut as an exhibition sport during the 1988 Calgary Games and became an official Olympic sport at the 1992 Games in Albertville, France.

He just figured he would couch-surf with a rotating list of friends and acquaintances.

Yuki eventually tracked down his son's whereabouts, but he did not set off to claim him right away, even though he was deeply concerned about Apolo's emotional state. Yuki knew his son was fuming, and he wanted to give Apolo some time to cool off. When Yuki finally knocked on the door of the home where his son was staying, Apolo would not listen to his father's pleas. Instead, he just stood there and refused to come home. Yuki felt ashamed and humiliated. He had been forced to go to another family's house to try to persuade his own son to come home. To this day, Yuki says it was easily one of the worst experiences of his life. Apolo's fury did not last much longer. The next day he had a change of heart and returned home. Apolo's rebellion had lasted a total of five days.

For the next week, Apolo and his father did a lot of talking. At one point, Yuki explained to his son that a person's friendships may last a short or long while, but relationships with family last forever. This notion struck Apolo with significance. Deep down, he was scared of losing his father's love and support. Finally, the pair came to an agreement. Apolo would go to Lake Placid and try the program for three months, from mid-July to mid-October. At that point, if he still wanted to come back to Washington, Yuki would welcome him home. This time Mr. Ohno did not take any chances and escorted Apolo all the way to Lake Placid.

DAYS IN LAKE PLACID

Apolo was unimpressed with the sleepy little town of Lake Placid, which, despite its small size and remote location in the Adirondack Mountains, had hosted two Winter Olympic Games—in 1932 during the Great Depression and in 1980. Apolo discovered that the Olympic village built for the 1980 Games was now being used as a medium-security prison. To

When he was 14, Apolo Ohno balked at joining a training program with the U.S. Junior National Development Team in Lake Placid, New York. After many fights with his father, Apolo finally went. For the teenager, the small town of Lake Placid *(above)* was quite a change from big-city Seattle.

the energetic teen, who was used to having lots of places to go and plenty to do in the Seattle area, Lake Placid itself seemed like a prison, too.

Upon his arrival, Apolo had little time to rest. His training began the very next morning, and it would not be easy. He was six weeks behind the other participants in the program. Since this was Apolo's first exposure to a true training program, he found the schedule grueling: Wake every day for a one-hour run at 7 A.M.; then go to skate practice for two hours; then do weight training for yet another two hours.

Early in the program, Coach Wentland shared with Yuki his feeling that Apolo held much promise as a short-track *(continues on page 32)*

Between the Generations

FROM ISOLATION TO IMMIGRATION

In the 1600s, Japanese leaders set a policy of isolationism to keep the influence of foreign nations from affecting their homeland. As part of this policy, Japanese citizens were not allowed to travel outside their country. Sentiment started to change in 1853, with the arrival of Commodore Matthew C. Perry of the U.S. Navy in Tokyo Harbor. Perry was instrumental in persuading the Japanese government to begin trade with the outside world.

Fifteen years later, Emperor Mutsuhito began his rule, another factor that would eventually influence Japanese immigration to the United States. During his Meiji era of "enlightened rule," which lasted until 1912, the emperor had a desire to strengthen his nation's military and economy. His solution was to tax his nation's farmers to raise the money he needed to accomplish his goals. At the same time, the emperor refused to raise the price of rice, the farmers' main crop, choosing to keep prices low. As a result, farmers soon began to lose money, and many eventually lost their farms.

In 1885, Japanese law officially allowed men and women to leave the country for foreign lands. That year was the start of a wave of Japanese immigration to Hawaii and California that lasted until 1924. Like many immigrants before them, the Japanese were inspired to leave by the promise of new jobs and higher wages. Of the 380,000 Japanese who came during that time, most were from southwest Japan. About 200,000 settled in Hawaii, with the other 180,000 moving to the West Coast of the United States.

These first-wave immigrants planned to stay in this new country only temporarily. They hoped that, after a few years of work, they would have saved enough money to make a proud return to Japan, pay off any debts, and buy back the farms they had lost. This earning power, though, became a temptation and was too valuable for many Japanese workers to give up, so they remained in the United States.

Japanese immigrants in Hawaii had an easier time becoming an accepted part of society, and by the 1920s, 43 percent of the Hawaiian population consisted of people of Japanese heritage. Immigrants to the U.S. mainland had a much harder time and faced discrimination. In fact, fear of these "outsiders" grew so intense that in 1924, the U.S. government passed a law that put a stop to all Japanese immigration.

As the first generation of immigrants born in Japan, or *Issei*, tried to make their way in this new homeland, they established their own businesses to serve their community. Believing that education could help the situation, they encouraged their children, or the *Nisei* generation, to study hard and aspire to white-collar occupations like that of doctor, engineer, scientist, or accountant.

A dark time in American history occurred in the early 1940s. On December 7, 1941, Japan bombed Pearl Harbor, Hawaii, and the following day the United States entered World War II by declaring war on Japan. Fear grew within the United States, and in February 1942 President Franklin D. Roosevelt signed an order that sent 120,000 people of Japanese heritage on the West Coast, whether Issei or Nisei, into internment camps complete with barbed-wire fences and armed guards. It was not until 1944 that the U.S. Supreme Court determined that this stripping of freedoms was unconstitutional.

The Issei and Nisei who suffered the indignity of these camps rarely talk about what happened there, but after regaining their freedom most remained in the United States to create further generations of Japanese Americans, the *Sansei* and their children, the *Yonsei*. The Issei paved the way for these later generations, and over the decades, Japanese Americans, like Apolo Anton Ohno, have made great contributions to American culture, growth, and achievement.

(continued from page 29)

skater, but Yuki was pessimistic. He was not sure his son would stay long enough to find out. When he called Apolo each week, pretty much all he heard were complaints. The food was bad. The schedule was repetitive. The routine was boring. On the phone with friends, Apolo kept telling them not to worry—he would be back in mid-October.

Apolo felt out of place. The teens in the program were mostly from the Midwest or the East Coast. There were no skaters from the West like him. When school started in September, he did not like it. Once again, he was easily bored as he had been as a younger child. This time, there was another reason for his dislike—there was no diversity in the public school. In his autobiography, Apolo says, "Everyone else was white, and although I'm a combination of Caucasian and Japanese, I've always considered myself Asian." There were no Latinos, and in the entire student body, there were only two African Americans and two Asians.

Eventually, Apolo did make a friend, and a great one at that. His name was Donald Stewart, and he went by the nickname "Crazy-D." Stewart was a dedicated athlete who took his skate training seriously, sometimes getting up at 3:00 in the morning to do an extra workout. He was a prankster as well, a trait that appealed to the fun-loving Apolo. The two were training partners and roommates, and for the most part, they both trained hard. But once in a while during a team run, Crazy-D and Apolo would stick to the back of the pack with one intention in mind—to cut out and jog down to the local pizza joint for a slice or two before hitching a ride back to the training center.

The friendship with Stewart made training camp bearable, and in spite of wanting to dislike anything and everything about his new situation, Apolo found another reason to stay—Coach Wentland. For Apolo, Wentland was his first true coach and trainer. Wentland came from the world of short-track skating and had many a victory under his belt. As a coach, he trained on the ice, right alongside his athletes. He had a contagious energy and commanded respect—Wentland was strict and intense, but he did not yell. His manner and methods appealed to the reluctant skater.

Within the first month, it was obvious to Apolo and the others that he was fast becoming one of the team's best skaters. This fact, though, worried the 14-year-old, who requested a chat with Wentland. Apolo was concerned that he might become too good too fast and burn out, but Wentland assured him this would not occur. He told Apolo he had nothing to worry about, except giving short track all that he had. In his autobiography, Apolo says that he ended the conversation by telling his coach, "Okay, then, I want you to make me a machine. I want to be the best ever. Make me a machine."

4

Big Wins, Big Disappointments

In August, only six weeks into Apolo Ohno's training at Lake Placid, the center was set to host a World Cup event. The competition would include a "Junior Exhibitions" special event, and Apolo had been handpicked as one of the U.S. representatives. This was a big deal for Apolo—it would be his debut with the Junior National Team. The race was scheduled for a Saturday. Unfortunately, Apolo suffered a setback the previous Tuesday when he took a spill on the ice because some sand had inadvertently gotten on the track by way of the rink's Zamboni. The fall was not pretty. Apolo hit the wall hard, knocking his hip out of joint. At first there was pain, but there was also numbness. Apolo could barely move and had to be helped off the ice by a trainer, who also had to pop the hip joint back into place. Yuki had come to visit Apolo, and neither he nor Apolo's trainers thought that he would be able to compete after such an injury. Apparently, everyone failed to anticipate the skater's drive and ambition to participate in such an important race.

Come Saturday, Apolo was obviously not at 100 percent. He walked with effort, and being on the ice caused intense pain. But once the determined skater was at the starting line, everything but the ice in front of him seemed to fade away. He was "in the zone" and ready for whatever his opponents had for him. In the end, Apolo overcame the pain, and the doubters, to win the exhibition—even with an injury. This certainly would not be the last time the spunky skater impressed observers with his determination and stamina in skating a great race.

Apolo did not go home after his three-month trial period ended, and by January 1997, when the Junior World Trials were being held, the skater felt that he was sure to make the team. That was until he hit the ice. The trials were taking place in Milwaukee, Wisconsin, and as soon as Apolo got onto the ice for practice, he felt that his blades were "off." Unfortunately, Apolo had only the one pair of blades. Both his father and Coach Wentland went to work on the skates to make minute adjustments, but no matter what they did, the skates just did not feel right to Apolo. This did not bode well for the competition. Blades help a skater make those crucial turns, and if those blades feel off, a skater's performance can be put on the line.

When race time came, Apolo gave his best effort, but the blades held him back. Despite the difficulties, he managed to pull out all the stops in his 1,000-meter race. He not only won, but he also broke the U.S. record. The race, though, was the only one in which he made the finals. Overall, he placed third, which may sound good, but it was not good enough. In the trials, only the top two U.S. skaters overall made it to the international team. Apolo had just missed out.

The situation left Apolo in a bad frame of mind. He felt entirely discouraged. He had put in so much hard work, and it seemed to him as if he had done it for nothing. Perhaps it was good that Apolo was riding back to upstate New York with his father, his most fervent supporter. Yuki tried to help Apolo

SHORT-TRACK GEAR

Because of the potential for injury in the fast and sometimes cata-clysmic world of short track, skaters wear protective gear on the ice, including guards, gloves, and helmets. Short trackers also wear special gear to help enhance their performance. This gear includes the body-hugging spandex "skinsuits" that make the competitors more aerodynamic. In addition, some skaters wear goggles to keep their eyes from streaming tears during short track's high-velocity skating. But the item of most importance to short-track athletes is their skates, with boots made of plastic in-stead of leather.

Skaters, like Apolo, devote a great deal of time to caring for the skates and blades that support them through the high speeds and ultra-tight turns of the short-track oval. A skater's relationship with his or her blades is almost like a more intense version of the "Princess and the Pea" fairy tale. It is crucial that a skater's blades feel just right, or the skater may not be able to glide in top form on the ice. Just a slight bend too much to the right or left can interfere with a skater's physical flow.

Apolo keeps his skating tool kit, filled with items like wrenches and special stones, in nothing more than a Tupper-ware container. Whenever Apolo senses an issue with his blades, he turns to his tool kit to solve the problem. A radius gauge, an extremely accurate device that can calculate mea-surements to 1/1,000 of an inch, helps him find the flaw, and then he uses a bender to crimp the blade a tiny distance. He checks the blade again with the radius gauge, goes back to work with the bender, and continues this process until the blade is where he needs it. He then uses a flat stone laced with diamond to smooth over the wear and tear the blade suffers on the ice. Finally, he uses smaller stones to smooth out the blade's sides.

focus on the positive. Despite a bad blade, Apolo had really come through and made a good showing. The young skater may not have had the outcome at the Junior World Trials that he had anticipated and desired, but he had shown that he could perform even with obstacles thrown in the way.

SENIOR SUCCESS

Yuki's inspirational talk seemed to reach Apolo, who went at his training even harder. Apolo knew that he was also eligible to compete at the senior level, so he set a new goal for himself: to race two months later at the 1997 Senior World Trials. The senior level proved to be a different experience for the ambitious skater. Now he was competing against world-class athletes, some of whom were Olympians. In these competitions, a nine-lap time trial is used to separate out the top 16 skaters—Apolo won this initial race. During the next race, a four-lap trial, Apolo took a spill on the ice, which usually means disaster as far as finishing a race, but the teen managed to get back up and keep going to tie for third. By the time Apolo made it into the actual races, he ranked first—ahead of seasoned Olympic skaters like Andrew Gabel, who was probably the best short-track speed skater at the time.

In the races that would determine Apolo's future, he again skated incredibly well. Although he did not place in the 1,000-meter race, he finished fourth in the 500 meters, second in the 3,000 meters, and first in the 1,500 meters. Unlike the Junior World Trials only two months before, this time Apolo had something tangible to show for all of his training. He won the overall title at the U.S. Senior World Trials and earned himself a place on the Senior World Team. Not only would he be training under Jeroen Otter with the Senior National Team in Colorado Springs, Colorado, he would be the No. 1 skater for his team in the World Cup. Second on the team would be Gabel.

Apolo's win did not necessarily sit well with many of the athletes who had been in training and on the circuit far longer than he had. As before in his life, Apolo felt like an outsider. Because of his relatively brief time in the sport, he was not a part of the speed-skating world's inner circle. An example of the chilly welcome Apolo received was the snub from the president of the U.S. speed-skating association. There was no doubt that Apolo had made an impressive showing at the senior trials, but despite his big victory, the association president did not bother to introduce himself to Apolo, congratulate him on his win, or even take the time to shake his hand.

Apolo's win meant that he would be training at the Olympic Training Center in Colorado Springs, but working out with a significantly older team proved a challenge. For starters, Coach Otter had never trained a 14-year-old, who might have different needs from those of the older skaters because his body was young and still growing, his mind young and still learning. Apolo's previous program was specifically tailored to the unique physical and psychological needs of younger athletes. In Colorado Springs, older skaters were expected to be more self-reliant. The team had no sports psychologist, and Apolo was not given any strict dietary plan. So the former latchkey kid fended for himself, eating whatever was available at the time, be it handfuls of candy or slices of leftover pizza.

So, not only was Apolo eating poorly, he was also trying to adjust to the new lifestyle of a senior skater. Sure, for many years he had traveled for his love of sports and competitions, but traveling was now at a whole new level. This was world travel, with day-and-night flights, jet lag, and adjustments to completely different climates—all factors that can take a toll on an athlete's stamina.

In the spring of 1997, world travel took the young skater to Japan for his first World Championships. There, at an arena in the city of Nagano, he found himself surrounded by athletes from around the globe, all at the top of their game. He soon discovered that international competitions differed greatly from the national competitions he was used to. Not only were the participants more intense, but they also had a tendency to skate closer together, forming tighter packs that left only small spaces between bodies. This made it much more difficult for skaters to pass their competitors.

This new and intense atmosphere became coupled with more blade issues for Apolo, who was forced to borrow a spare pair of skates from a teammate. The results were fairly disastrous for someone in the No. 1 position on his team.

Apolo made his way into the finals of the 1,000 meters but ultimately did not place. His performances in the 1,500- and 3,000-meter races were even worse—he did not make the finals of either event. By the end of the Nagano competition, the formerly confident skater found himself placing 19th overall and feeling exhausted. The whole experience had been a huge disappointment.

A MUCH-NEEDED BREAK

Still contending with the disappointment of Nagano, Apolo implored his father to let him take a break. Yuki could see that his son was distraught and agreed that he should take some time away from the stress of training in Colorado Springs. Coach Otter told Apolo what he needed to do to stay in shape while he was away. Unfortunately, Apolo ignored his coach's advice and suggestions, making a conscious choice not to even get on a bike.

Now, finally, here was that summer vacation Apolo had longed for. From April to August, he traded in his long days and endless hours of training and workouts for sleeping in, lazing about the beach, and munching away on BBQ and his old favorite, pizza. In short track, it is normal for some skaters to take a bit of a break, to reduce their level of training in the

Known for his focus and preparation, Apolo Ohno *(second from right)* trained with his teammates before a World Cup event in October 2008 in Vancouver, British Columbia. In 1997, though, during his first year on the Senior World Team, Apolo suffered a disappointing result at the World Championships. He took some time off but failed to train. When he returned to the team, he was 15 pounds overweight, and his skating suffered.

months of June and July. Apolo, though, took this to a whole new level. It would not take long for him to learn that no workouts and no ice time meant no glory.

After spending time away from short track that summer, Apolo returned to the sport and attended a training camp in Chamonix, France. His 5-foot-8 (173-centimeter) frame was now carrying an extra 15 pounds (6.8 kilograms), and Apolo had a hard time keeping up with his teammates. Back on his regimen of biking, weight training, and running, Apolo realized that he was out of shape. On top of that, he came down with a bad case of the flu. Apolo was having such a difficult time in France because of his illness that Otter sent him home to recuperate for two-and-a-half weeks before training was to start up again in Colorado Springs. The coach again encouraged Apolo to at least bike hard during those weeks, but again Apolo failed to follow Otter's instructions. Eventually, the young skater would learn his lesson the hardest of ways.

FATEFUL OLYMPIC TRIALS

After his return to Colorado Springs in the fall of 1997, Apolo felt as if he had a bull's-eye on his back. Teammates and competitors alike were looking to knock Apolo from the top spot. Many could not accept that such a young skater was the leader at this level of competition.

Around this time, Apolo began to take creatine, a legal performance and muscle enhancer that a lot of skaters were using. The substance seemed to work at first, helping Apolo gain several pounds of muscle and feel stronger. Within another month, though, Apolo had added even more weight, and he often felt tired and sluggish instead of energized. He became sick again and had to take another round of antibiotics—something he dreaded, since they usually had a negative effect on his performance. At the request of his coaches, Apolo, still ailing, took part in the U.S. Junior Short Track Championships. He placed second overall, but his body and mind felt completely worn out.

Apolo was in rough shape. On the senior circuit, he had been plagued by sickness; had less contact with his support system—his father—than ever before; had to contend with the stress of constant international travel and competition; and found himself in a world that did not seem to understand the needs of a young skater. While under Coach Wentland, Apolo and his team regularly practiced time trials. With this new team and new set of coaches, however, Apolo had done only a few—a change that would prove fatal to his career. In hindsight, Apolo says what happened next was not all his coaches' fault. Sure, they did not seem to understand his needs, but the coaches needed to look out for an entire team, not just one member of it. Apolo said he should have spoken up for himself and voiced how he felt.

Only a few weeks later, it was January 1998 and the all-important Olympic Trials. For any skater, these two weeks are crucial. Races are held on Fridays and Saturdays, with the other five days left for practice and rest. On the first weekend, Apolo had a nine-lap time trial scheduled. The points from the time trial would be added to points received during other races at the Olympic Trials—that is, as long as points were earned. The strain of the last several months finally came to a breaking point at the worst possible moment. Apolo received zero points in his nine-lap trial, and to make matters worse, he did not qualify for even one of that weekend's finals. The following weekend proved equally disastrous for the skater from Seattle. In the four-lap time trial, Apolo did not receive a single point, and again, he did not take part in any finals. Apolo later reflected on the experience on Olympics.com, "Everybody was expecting me to make the Nagano Olympic Team and expecting me to go and get a medal. And in my mind, I had no expectations at all. I wasn't ready for the Olympic Trials at all. I was overweight.

I hadn't been training; my technique was horrible. Mentally, I didn't even care."

The skater who had shown so much promise to make the top spot on the senior team had just finished 16th out of 16 in the Olympic Trials. There would be no Olympic Games, let alone Olympic glory, for Apolo Anton Ohno.

5

Apolo Gets Serious

There was no question, the Olympic Trials had been a disaster, and as a result Apolo Ohno was devastated. Yuki was furious with his son's coaches and the skating federation, feeling that they had let Apolo down by not making adjustments to help the 15-year-old. Apolo, though, took the blame solely upon himself. This was his failure, no one else's.

This disappointment was the final straw. When Apolo saw his former coach, Pat Wentland, he flat out told him this was the end—he was going to quit skating. Wentland tried his best to provide encouragement; he still had faith in the young athlete. The coach did not argue with Apolo's desire to return home, but he advised him not to make such a rash decision in the heat of such tumultuous feelings. He recommended that Apolo continue to train while at home and give careful thought to his future as a skater. Wentland's words fell on deaf ears. Apolo was determined to let it all go.

CABIN FEVER

Yuki, who could often help his son see the rational side of situations, wanted to help Apolo find his way through this difficult time. He placed no pressure on his son to choose to continue skating, but he did want Apolo to make a decision. He wanted him to put careful thought into the direction he wanted his life to take. For this, Yuki had a plan.

Almost as soon as father and son returned home to Seattle, Yuki drove Apolo out to the isolated spot at the Iron Springs Resort in Copalis Beach and the cabin where they had spent so much quality time together. The catch was that Yuki did not stay. Apolo was left alone with only his cat, Tiggie, for company. With no phone or stereo and the nearest town a 25-minute walk away, the cottage had little to offer but time for contemplation.

For the first few days, Apolo had just the rain, his thoughts, and a lot of time on the stationary bike he had brought along. On day three, January 21, he began to write a journal, noting that he would need to keep his faith in God, his father, and himself if he did decide to continue with competitive skating. At one point that day, Apolo considered walking down the road to the pay phone to call his father for a ride back home. But something told him the time wasn't right—he needed more time alone. Though it was bleak, gray, and raining outside, Apolo decided to go for a run, a move that started a new daily regimen for the isolated athlete. On day four, he started with a long morning run, biked intensely during the day, and took a break to watch skating tapes on the tiny TV he brought with him. He ended his routine with another run in the evening.

Day four also marked the turning point in the skater's life. While out on one of his runs, he stopped at a boulder to tend to a blister on his foot. There, the conflicted teen tended to his thoughts as well. He looked deep inside himself for his motivation. He did not think it likely that short track would bring him fame or fortune, so why should he devote his next four years to the sport and another shot at the Olympics? And the answer seemed so plain—because he loved it, because he was exhilarated by it, even during the hard times. The nine-day trip had made all the difference in the world. Apolo now knew what he wanted. He wanted short track, and he wanted success.

THE BEGINNING OF A NEW APOLO

Because of timing—the coaches from Colorado Springs were still away with the other skaters at the 1998 Nagano Olympics—Apolo returned to Lake Placid to train. His enthusiasm was helped along by a friend, Mike Kooreman, who had not made the Olympic team either. Kooreman was excited about the 1998 World Cup Team Trials, and his fervor rubbed off on Apolo, who now took his workouts seriously. He filled his days with running, weight training, and 90-minute bike sessions of hard-core sprint and interval training. At Lake Placid, Apolo was also introduced to a new junior coach named John Monroe, who was worried that Apolo was pushing himself too hard. In fact, after one especially intense bike workout, Apolo passed out in a hallway. But the newly dedicated skater was determined to make a comeback—nothing would stop him now.

In March, the World Cup Team Trials were held in Marquette, Michigan. The competition was important because it would decide who would become World Team members and who would be eligible to compete in the 1998–1999 World Cup races. At the event, Apolo was a bit unsure of himself, but he tried not to let that show. In the end, his skating triumphed over any self-doubts. He skated well enough to earn the fifth and final spot on the team. The new World Team member realized he would not see a lot of action as the team's alternate, but this time he set any discouraging thoughts aside—telling himself to be thankful he was on the team at all. This complacency did not last long, however. Apolo was hungry to be back in that No. 1 spot. He wanted to be a machine again.

Apolo decided not to return to Colorado Springs until he had built up more confidence and strength. Instead, he headed to Seattle, where he and Yuki set up a makeshift training center in the garage. There, for three months, Apolo spent two hours a day on a stationary bike, multitasking by watching himself and competitors on videos while he pedaled. He may not have had ice time, but he did strike a balance with resistance training and dry-land workouts. He was eating better, too, cutting out all fat from his diet. All of his efforts seemed to be paying off: Apolo was getting lean and increasing his strength and endurance. During this time, Apolo also helped build his confidence through education. The local school system set him up with an online program called the Internet Academy that allowed Apolo to have a lot of contact with the instructors and go at his own pace.

A NEW INFLUENCE

By the time Apolo returned to Colorado Springs, his body was transformed. Now, during high-altitude runs and team bike rides, Apolo led the pack. Pat Wentland was now the head coach in Colorado. Both he and the team members were taking notice of the new-and-improved Apolo.

The teen athlete's real breakthrough was yet to come. Wentland had invited a 21-year-old student at Colorado College with a keen interest in sports psychology to be his team's resident adviser. The student's name was Dave Creswell, and although Apolo did not feel any special connection to him at first, Creswell and his philosophies and techniques were soon to make a huge impact on Apolo and his skating. During games of badminton (the U.S. Olympic Badminton Team trains in Colorado Springs, too), Creswell, whose skill at tennis made him a more than worthy opponent for Apolo, would pose questions to the young athlete—like, Why did certain things happen in the game the way they did? Over time, Apolo's badminton game improved, and he thought there just might be something to sports psychology after all.

Soon, the two started to go for runs through a scenic area of red rock in the northern mountains of Colorado Springs known as the "Garden of the Gods." On these runs, Creswell began to talk to Apolo about alternative techniques like meditation and centering and breathing exercises. The old Apolo may have been skeptical of such methods, but the new Apolo respected and trusted Creswell, so he paid careful attention to what he had to say. In time, Apolo implemented these strategies as ways to relax when facing the pain and fatigue caused by the physical strain of his sport. He even found himself doing centering exercises while in the bathtub. Eventually, Creswell taught him how to use these same techniques and exercises during practice on the ice and when out on the road. Finally, Apolo's new friend showed him the benefits of using the same exercises while sitting in the heat box—where skaters wait during races—and out on the ice itself. Apolo used all of Creswell's techniques during his few opportunities to compete on the ice during the 1998–1999 World Cup season, and they proved more than useful.

Apolo did not see much action in the first three World Cup events, but that changed when he had the chance to compete in individual races at the fourth World Cup event in Hungary. There, Apolo was up against the best of the best—Kim Dong-Sung, a South Korean who had won gold at the Nagano Olympics; Fabio Carta of Italy; and Canada's Marc Gagnon, a four-time world champion. Hungary was also where Apolo enjoyed the thrill of his first World Cup win. He flew past Carta and Kim in the final turn to place first in the 1,000 meters. Not only had he won, but he had also become the youngest skater to win that particular race in a World Cup series. The kid from Seattle had performed so well

APOLO'S HEROES AND INSPIRATIONS

Many kids today look at Apolo Anton Ohno as a role model or a hero. Throughout his life, Apolo has had heroes of his own. Sports legend Muhammad Ali is one of those people Apolo strongly admires. As a kid, Apolo would visit a bookstore to read up on the boxing champ, and in school, all of Apolo's book reports had one focus: the three-time heavyweight champion of the world, Ali. Even as an adult, Apolo still reveres his childhood idol, viewing him as even more of a role model given Ali's work on behalf of Parkinson's disease.

Another athlete Apolo looks up to is multiple Tour de France winner Lance Armstrong. Apolo admires the courage the biker displayed in his battle against testicular cancer, which spread to his lungs, abdomen, and brain. Armstrong not only went on to recover, but he also got to the top of his sport, winning the grueling Tour de France bike race a record seven consecutive times.

In Ali and Armstrong, Apolo recognizes their innate talent, but what he finds most admirable is their dedication and passion— they have truly given their sports their all.

Another of the skater's role models is his first real coach, Pat Wentland, who trained Apolo when he reluctantly joined the U.S. Junior National Development Team in Lake Placid, New York. Apolo remains indebted to Wentland for his faith in such a young and strong-willed skater and for his imminent skill as a coach, remarking on Wentland's ability to make him a champion in only one year's time. The skater says in his autobiography, "I respect and value his opinions to this day."

But perhaps Apolo's biggest hero is his father, Yuki. Although they have had their ups and downs, their relationship has always been close. Apolo has often said that his father is his partner in short track and a powerful influence on decisions about skating and about living life. Apolo says his father has sacrificed much to get him to the top.

that he ranked third overall. The experience was a boon to his confidence—Apolo was definitely back in the game.

THE JUNIOR WORLD CHAMPIONSHIPS

Next up was the Junior World Championships in Montreal, Canada. Once again, Apolo put into play the techniques Creswell had taught him, incorporating positive self-talk and affirmations as well as visualization into his routine. Creswell even took Apolo into the empty arena to breathe, plan, and imagine the event's outcome.

By no means was the skating easy. In his autobiography, Apolo says that the Koreans "played some weird games" on the ice. Their more obvious methods—such as having a coach blow a whistle from the sidelines whenever a South Korean was about to be passed by another skater—were not illegal, but they were distracting. Apolo was pretty certain, however, that the Koreans also were using a subtler maneuver called team skating, which is illegal in short track. Team skating happens when an entire team works together, skating in a manner to help one specific member win a race. The technique is incredibly difficult to prove, and thus no accusations were made during the Junior World Championships.

The situation made it even tougher than usual for Apolo to skate his way to a victory. Everything came down to the 1,500-meter race. Apolo knew he had to win this event to capture the overall title at the championships. The Koreans put in a tough fight during their laps around the ice, but in the end, Apolo's hard work, perseverance, and newly found alternative techniques helped him make it across the finish line first. He had won the Junior World Title and again had set a record as the youngest ever to achieve the title. This accomplishment was exactly what he needed to rebuild the confidence he had lost. He felt more certain than ever that this was the mark of his comeback.

A TROUBLESOME BACK

After his 1999 Junior World Championships win, Apolo continued to compete in events around the globe like the World Short Track Speed Skating Championships in Bulgaria, where he won silver in the 500 meters and placed fourth overall, despite his back giving him some trouble.

He had taken a spill some weeks earlier during a 500-meter race in the World Team Championships in St. Louis, Missouri.

Apolo Anton Ohno *(right)* took on Li Jiajun *(center)* of China and Fabio Carta *(left)* of Italy in the 500-meter race at the 1999 World Short Track Speed Skating Championships in Bulgaria. Apolo finished second in the race and fourth overall in the championships. He was beginning to make his mark in world competition.

While trying to catch Canadian skater François-Louis Trem-blay, Apolo had the misfortune of having his blade hit one of the blocks. (There are seven small rubber blocks set up to mark the turns.) He went down immediately, hitting the rink wall in the process. The coach yelled for Apolo to get back up and finish the race. The American team desperately needed the points to maintain its lead, and if Apolo did not finish the race, the team would receive no points at all. Apolo managed to pull himself back up and skate to the finish, but the fall had done its damage. With his chest hurting and his middle and upper back in tremendous pain, Apolo was pulled from the rest of the competition. His trainers said he had bruised the bones in his back. It was not until much later that Apolo found out he had done much worse than that.

SKATING THROUGH PAIN

In August 1999, Apolo, like many top athletes, took a little time off between seasons. Back home in Seattle, he continued his regimen of three workouts a day, even though he often felt pain and discomfort. He knew athletes' bodies were prone to taking a beating, so he shrugged it off, believing the pain to be just normal wear and tear on the body.

When the new season started up again, however, Apolo found himself plagued not only with pain, but also with ill-ness. He certainly had high points, like his first experi-ence of feeding off the energy of a large crowd at the rink in Changchun, China—which had a capacity of 12,000 spectators. There, Apolo exploded onto the ice, feeling the excitement of the avid Chinese fans. In this World Cup event, he placed first overall. Once again, it was a huge victory: He was the young-est skater ever to win a World Cup title. On his way to taking the title, Apolo had beaten China's famed top skater, Li Jiajun, which made Apolo an instant celebrity in the country. Here he felt his first touch of fame, being asked for interviews and being recognized while out and about. It was another exciting moment for Apolo, but the situation was not entirely rosy. He was catching almost every manner of illness around, so for the next few months, Apolo skipped some of the less crucial events on the short-track calendar.

During the course of the season, short track took its toll on the skater. At the U.S. Championships in Boston that February, Apolo did well, placing first in the 1,500 meters. The 1,000-meter race, though, took him out completely when he hit a wall, causing him to dislocate both kneecaps. As the pain burned through his legs, the tough skater managed to pop one kneecap back into place while still on the ice. Immediately after the race, Yuki drove his son to the nearest hospital emergency room. Although the competition was not over when he got hurt, Apolo had earned enough points to place second overall, easily but painfully making the U.S. National Team.

By the time of the World Championships in Sheffield, England, Apolo was so sick that Yuki traveled with him. Doctors had discovered that the teen's red-blood-cell count was well below normal and his white-blood-cell count was running high. Apolo managed to compete with a 102-degree (39-degree Celsuis) fever and a constant, hacking cough. He was again on antibiotics, but he skated as best as he could, given the circumstances. Unfortunately, the illness was racking his body—he did not come close to a win; his best performance was seventh in one race.

Reflecting on these events, Apolo said the never-ending sickness was certainly part of his trouble, but another factor was Coach Susan Ellis, who had replaced Coach Wentland when he was let go from the team. She placed a great deal of emphasis on weight training and less on cardiovascular exercise. With these workouts, Apolo did develop more muscle in his legs, pressing 1,500 pounds (680 kilograms), but the cost was added weight, even if it was muscle. Apolo had power, but the 20 extra pounds

(9 kilograms) on his body made it harder for him to get back into form after each race.

NOT MUCH OF A SUMMER BREAK

Apolo knew what he had to do—more cardio and less weight training. So over the summer, he implemented a new workout schedule to prepare his body for the 2000–2001 season. All of the other skaters left Colorado Springs and went home during the summer, but Apolo chose to remain at the training facility because he did not want to give up that all-important ice time. Apolo was not completely on his own there. Even though he was no longer Apolo's coach, Wentland wanted to help the young skater, and the two went on runs along with Wentland's wife four times each week. The tough schedule of intense StairMaster workouts, private ice time, lengthy runs, and high-altitude bike rides paid off. Within two months, Apolo was weighing in at an ideal 158 pounds (72 kilograms), and within three months his blood count was back to normal.

The work paid off in other ways as well. Apolo's 2000–2001 World Cup season started off with a bang late that October in Calgary, Canada. He had a new finely tuned body and a finely tuned mindset. Apolo used Creswell's techniques and envisioned himself skating to victory in every race. The young skater pulled it off and placed first in three events, the 500, the 1,000, and the 1,500 meters, skating past seasoned pros like Gagnon, Kim, and his Chinese nemesis Li, and earning their respect and congratulations on the way—Apolo had managed to set U.S. records in the 500 and 1,500 meters.

The next World Cup event was held in Provo, Utah, and again Apolo made a good showing, coming in second overall. He noticed something interesting, too—short track was receiving more media attention. And at one press conference, Apolo seemed to be the reporters' main focus, which he did not mind since the attention was all so positive.

Apolo Anton Ohno *(left)* and Kim Dong-Sung of South Korea fought for position around a corner during the 1,500-meter final in a World Cup event in December 2000 in Japan. Apolo ended the 2000–2001 World Cup season as the overall leader.

At the season's World Cup event in China, Apolo captured the overall title, for the second consecutive year. There was no question: Apolo's short track was on the right track. But the seemingly unstoppable skater's biggest accomplishment was yet to come. In Austria, at the final World Cup event of the season, the skater from Seattle again gave it his all. He not only won the finals in the 500-, 1,500-, and 3,000-meter races, but he also took home the gold for each of these distances for the entire year. On top of that, he captured the season's overall title. It was now clear: In the realm of short-track speed skating, no one could question the force of Apolo Anton Ohno.

6

Commitment and Controversy

U nfortunately, Apolo Ohno's glory at the World Cup was soon marred by intense back pain. In March 2001, he traveled to Japan for the World Team Championships. While working out with some light weights before the competition, Ohno felt something go horribly wrong in his back—a hot, deep pain that caused him to lose his breath. The races would not take place for a few days, so his trainers, not quite certain what was wrong, recommended the standard treatment—ice, massage, and rest.

Come race time, Ohno made his way onto the ice but not without suffering. He managed a first-place finish in the 3,000 meters, but during the race his back had gone into spasms. Ohno considered asking to be pulled from the competition because of the pain and weakness he was feeling, but he knew his team needed him. He alerted Coach Susan Ellis to his condition but continued to skate. Ohno's poor physical state was taking its toll.

PUSHING PAST THE PAIN

The determined short-track skater tried to push the pain aside for the World Championships held the very next week in South Korea. This competition was the biggest of the year and Ohno's first opportunity to make good in the senior World Championships. The outcome, however, was not what Ohno wanted. In the 1,500-meter final, he placed fourth, and the 500 meters was a total bust. He recovered a bit in the 1,000 meters, placing second but losing any shot at the championship's overall title.

Apolo Ohno held the lead during the 5,000-meter relay final at the 2001 World Championships in South Korea. A back injury hampered Ohno during the competition, but he still managed to finish second overall. His injury, though, would take him off the ice for months.

Everything came down to the 3,000-meter event. If Ohno took first, he would place second overall, with Marc Gagnon placing third overall. But if Gagnon finished before either Ohno or Li Jiajun, then the Canadian would take the overall title and his fifth gold in the World Championships. The competition in this event was fierce, but even in his diminished physical capacity, Ohno blazed across the ice and pulled out a win, capturing silver for the overall title.

Through his spring training in Colorado, Ohno kept on going even though his body still vibrated pain. Ohno's usual training routine included skating laps while wearing a weight vest. Normally, he could easily do 60 laps. Now, he could barely do 20, and that was without the vest. Looking back, Ohno says he should have learned by then to listen to his body, but he was consumed with remaining in top physical condition—so consumed in fact that he pushed himself hard to get back up to his usual 60 laps and refused to stop there. Although the back pain was increasingly getting worse, the determined skater pushed himself all the way to 80 laps.

This physical triumph did not last long. By May 2001, the spasms were so bad that Ohno could not even get through an entire practice. He knew it was finally time to seek help. He went to a local chiropractor, and after X-rays and an MRI, he was diagnosed with facet syndrome in his lower back. This is a condition in which the joints in the back of the spine degenerate so much that they cause pain. Additionally, Ohno had muscle tears and a bulging disc in his lower back that caused pain to radiate into his legs. The chiropractor, Dr. Scott Rosenquist, told the athlete that he would need a minimum of eight weeks of rehabilitation just to get back on the ice; he would need three months to reach an 80 percent recovery level. And there was no guarantee the physical therapy would work. There was a chance Ohno would need surgery. The diagnosis was a blow to Ohno, since the Olympic Trials were only seven months away.

For the next three months, Ohno concentrated on physical therapy and recovering. By August, the restless skater returned to the ice to begin to train for the trials. Ohno knew that skating was as much a mental game as a physical one, and he could not appear to be weak. So, no matter how he felt physically, he attended every practice, bowing out early only when the pain told him he had to.

By October, Ohno was still 15 percent away from a complete recovery, but he felt it imperative that he skate and decided to participate in the World Cup event in Calgary, Alberta, Canada. At his chiropractor's request, Ohno had pulled out of the World Cup season's first events. With his absence, rumors had started to circulate that the wonder kid from Seattle was not going to make it to the 2002 Olympic Games. With the trials only two months away, Ohno was determined to show everyone that he was back in the game. He took first in the 1,000 meters and second in the 3,000 meters in Calgary.

THE OLYMPIC TRIALS

For a country to get into the Olympics in various sports, its athletes must prove their mettle in a round of pre-Olympic events known as the World Qualifiers. The results of these competitions determine not only which countries can participate in the Olympic Games, but also how many athletes each nation can bring to that event. Although Ohno was unhappy with his performance at the World Qualifiers, he did secure his chance to compete in individual events at the Olympic Trials. It had been a hard road, but Ohno was now one step closer to skating in the Olympic Games that had been his inspiration.

Life soon became a whirlwind for Ohno. He was training six, sometimes seven, times a week, and with the Olympics on the horizon, his agents were busy scheduling interviews with the likes of *Sports Illustrated* and *GQ* magazines as well as meetings for sponsorship opportunities. Ohno was especially

Chased by Kim Dong-Sung of South Korea, Apolo Anton Ohno skated to victory in the 1,000-meter race in October 2001 at the World Cup event in Calgary, Alberta. The competition marked Ohno's return to the ice after undergoing months of physical therapy and rehabilitation on his back.

excited about the latter. Training at the top level of any sport is not cheap, and for all these years, Yuki had been shouldering the cost alone. Ohno saw sponsorships as a way to earn money to support his own training, therefore alleviating the burden on Yuki. He also saw sponsorships as a way to boost the profile of short track, the sport he loved. What Ohno could not know was that, within a short period of time, his sponsorships, and more important, his entire skating career would be placed in jeopardy.

The World Qualifiers had determined that the United States would indeed compete in short track at the Olympics.

The Olympic Trials, on the other hand, would determine which athletes would compete in Salt Lake City as members of the U.S. National Team.

These two weeks of competition in December were crucial for Ohno. His personal goal was to finish as one of the top two skaters at each distance and secure his place to compete in all four Olympic short-track events. To avoid the distraction of mind games and chitchat with other skaters and to maintain an inward focus, Ohno chose to stay at a separate hotel from the rest of his teammates. In his autobiography, he explained, "At Olympic Trials, I don't talk to anyone—I'm very quiet, focused, and in my own zone before a race. Short track is an individual sport, and you can't be friends on the ice. It won't work."

CHAMPION FOR A CAUSE

With his unexpected fame, Apolo Ohno has felt it important to give back to the community. His strong convictions led him to participate in Gap's (PRODUCT) RED campaign, created by U2 lead singer Bono and Kennedy family member Bobby Shriver. The campaign, a merging of fashion and activism, hopes to eliminate the plague of AIDS in Africa.

To get attention for (PRODUCT) RED and its cause, an advertising campaign was launched using a string of celebrities wearing their favorite (PRODUCT) RED items, like a T-shirt or a hoodie, as captured by famed photographer Annie Leibovitz. Each ad also featured one word ending in "-red," such as *inspi(red),* to describe the person featured. Ohno was among the first celebrities to take part. In his ad, he wore a (PRODUCT) RED headband and across his photo read the word *Endu(red).* Ohno's photo, along with those of Chris Rock, Steven Spielberg, Don Cheadle, and Mary J. Blige, appeared in magazines like *Vanity Fair; O, The Oprah Magazine;* and *Vogue.*

Ohno aced his way through the series of preliminaries, heats, quarterfinals, and semifinals that led to the finals for each race distance. Along the way, he racked up a number of first-place finishes. In the 500 meters, he won every heat and in the final managed to set a new U.S. record with a time of 41.628 seconds. He set a world record in the 1,500 meters with a time of 2 minutes, 13.728 seconds. By Saturday, December 22, and the trials' final event, the 1,000 meters, Ohno had earned 6,909 points, enough to ensure that he made the team and would race in the individual events at the Games. Knowing his position was secure, and wary of further injury to his back or the risk of any new injury, Ohno planned to play it safe, even telling reporters that his health was more important than a sweeping win at the trials.

A SHADOW FALLS

The controversy that made headlines happened when Ohno failed to win the 1,000-meter final. For most of the race, Shani Davis was ahead, which should have been no surprise. He owned this distance, having set a U.S. record in it only a few months before. In second place was Rusty Smith, with Ohno skating behind. While circling the track, another skater tried to pass Ohno poorly, and Ohno almost went down—a reminder to stick to his safety mantra. Davis skated across the finish line first, which garnered him a place on the Olympic team. He would be the first African American to skate on the U.S. Winter Olympic team. Smith finished second, and Ohno placed third. At the time, no complaints or disqualifications were made, and the referees certified the race and its results. Elated for his friend, Ohno congratulated Davis with a hug, an act of con-geniality and sportsmanship that would soon be used against him.

After the trials, Ohno took off for Los Angeles with his father for a Nike commercial and photo shoot. While there, he missed the post-trials dinner celebrating the team, but amid the celebration, whispers and rumors were starting to spread. When Ohno arrived back in Colorado Springs, he was greeted by the screaming headlines of local newspapers telling of a growing controversy surrounding the trials. He also came home to hundreds of messages requesting his side of the story.

What had happened was that another teammate, Tommy O'Hare (a 1998 Olympian whom Ohno now refers to only as the "roach"), claimed that the 1,000-meter final had been fixed by Ohno and Smith, who allegedly conspired to get their friend Davis onto the team. On December 27, O'Hare filed an offi-

During the 1,000-meter race at the U.S. Olympic Trials in December 2001, Apolo Anton Ohno glanced over at the leader, Shani Davis (far left). Between them was Rusty Smith. Setting off a controversy right before the Olympic Games, another speed skater accused Smith and Ohno of fixing the 1,000-meter race so that Davis would win and make the Olympic team.

cial complaint and demand for arbitration. The accusation was serious. At the least, it could cause Ohno and his friends to lose sponsorships from companies wary of having their products associated with scandal. At the most, they could face a ban from competition in their sport altogether.

VINDICATION

In response to O'Hare's action, Smith filed a defamation suit against his accuser on January 17, claiming that the other skater's allegations were damaging his reputation. With the Olympic Games less than a month away, Ohno did his best to lie low, choosing to concentrate on skating rather than getting sucked into the world of vicious accusations and inquisitive reporters. But focus was difficult. The story surrounded him everywhere, and he could not help but be upset when he saw shoddy journalism and fabricated quotations.

Ohno refused to enter the fray by talking to the media, at the time making only one official statement regarding the incident: "With a near-fall four laps before the end of the race, I decided to play it safe and protect my place in the 1,000 meters for the Olympic Games. I've said since the moment I learned of the accusations that they were untrue and I did nothing wrong. This unfortunate situation and the questioning of my character by a few specific people has been trying. But I am completely focused on winning gold for the U.S. in Salt Lake next month."

The arbitration took place at the U.S. Olympic Committee headquarters in Colorado Springs. Among the written statements and testimony given was mention of that congratulatory hug Ohno had given Davis, only now it was being described as a tainted act that had "implied wrongdoing." Several witnesses came forward to say that they overheard details of the race being fixed, and one referee who had certified the race now said he had concerns about its integrity. But within three days, before Ohno's and Smith's witnesses even made it to the stand, something remarkable happened. The sworn statements of the men's critics fell apart when their obvious inconsistencies were made apparent during cross-examination.

As a result of this courtroom debacle, O'Hare dropped his complaint, and afterward, Smith dropped his defamation suit. But the sport of short-track speed skating had been scarred. To try to heal that wound, Ohno's and Smith's lawyers insisted that the arbitrator, James Holbrook, issue his finding to put a conclusive end to the matter. In his statement on January 25, Holbrook said there was no evidence to support the accusation of a conspiracy to fix the race. Specifically, he stated: "Neither Ohno, Smith, nor Davis violated the rules or code of conduct of the U.S. Speedskating, the USOC [United States Olympic Committee], or the International Skating Union. Some statements in the submitted affidavits were admittedly inaccurate and there is no evidence submitted which would support any finding that the race had been fixed."

Ohno had been vindicated. He was now on his way to the Olympics.

The Beauty of Silver and Gold

By the time the 2002 Winter Olympics arrived, U.S. speed-skating coach Susan Ellis called short track "the hottest ticket in town." And indeed it was, selling out the 16,500 seats at the Salt Lake Ice Center. The race-fixing controversy may have proven the saying that there's no such thing as bad publicity.

In the months leading up to the Games, Apolo Anton Ohno was getting noticed, too. NBC, which was televising the Olympics in the United States, particularly gave a lot of attention to the little-known sport of short track and a certain rising star, Ohno. NBC sports commentator Ted Robinson spoke enthusiastically about the Seattle native's abilities on the ice: "Ohno is a magician on skates, able to do things on blades that his coach, Susan Ellis, says not even figure skaters can execute." Ohno credits the network for the outpouring of support he received during the Games.

All the attention may have meant added pressure to anyone else: Commentators and fans were touting Ohno as the U.S. athlete most likely to win the most medals. Many people were hoping that he would take gold in all four of his events. Ohno was aware of people's hopes, telling *Sports Illustrated for Kids,* "The expectation to win is pretty high. But to come prepared is the only thing I can control. . . . What happened in 1998 [not making the Olympic team] makes me hungrier to do well in 2002."

A POSSIBLE SETBACK

Upon arriving in Salt Lake City, Ohno had to get his official Olympic Games identification cards. With those in hand, he was off to a huge warehouse filled with all kinds of apparel and accessories embroidered with U.S.A. and the five-ringed Olympic insignia. The opening ceremony claimed 52,000 in attendance with millions upon millions of people watching from around the world. Almost in disbelief, Ohno looked on as famous performers like Sting, the Dixie Chicks, and cellist Yo-Yo Ma took the stage. He had finally made it. He was actually here.

Unfortunately, as had happened in the past before important competitions, Ohno came down with a terrible case of the flu only days before his first event. He was so sick that he was moved from the Olympic Village, where almost all the athletes stay, to a hotel closer to the Salt Lake Ice Center.

By the time of the preliminaries for his first short-track event, Ohno was somewhat better. He soon forgot about the coughing and sniffling when he stepped into the arena and heard his name being chanted by throngs of fans he did not even know he had.

AN EVENTFUL 1,000-METER RACE

During the first qualifying rounds for the 1,000-meter event, Ohno's confidence on the ice was recognized by spectators, reporters, and fellow athletes alike. But the person Ohno had to beat was Chinese skater Li Jiajun, who was the previous year's world champion in the 1,000 meters. Anyone watching closely saw Ohno yawn as he approached the starting line that Saturday night for the final and his first shot at an Olympic medal. What could have been interpreted as a laidback attitude would not last long, however. Once the race began, Ohno was giving it his all and setting the pace for the first eight laps around the oval.

In the final turn, Ohno was in the lead and the one to beat. Without much room on the outside, Li tried to gain an edge and pass Ohno. What happened next was a smashup of spectacular proportions. When Li made his move to pass the race leader, Ohno put out his right hand in an attempt to push him off (a legal move in the sport). Ohno's quick response put his challenger off balance, which created a domino effect. Skating behind the two men were 16-year-old South Korean Ahn Hyun-Soo, who went down along with Li. The young South Korean took out Canadian skater Mathieu Turcotte, who in turn sent Ohno into a 360-degree spin, back first into the boards on his way down to the cold, hard ice.

Li did not recover from his fall, but Ohno, feeling light-headed and with his ears humming from the hard knock he just took, surprised everyone by crawling on his side to cross the finish line. Seeing the determined Ohno, Turcotte followed suit, making a last-minute baseball-like slide to cross the finish line himself. For both men, it was too late. Australian Steven Bradbury, who had been in last place during the entire race and was ranked 35th in the world in the 1,000 meters, had lucked out and avoided the four-skater pileup, breezing past the chaos to win gold.

Many people were incensed by Bradbury's win, and his victory lap was marred by boos and one fan who kept screaming that he did not deserve the gold medal. The fan's protests were enough to provoke Bradbury into exchanging expletives with him. Ohno had a lot of fans and publicity and he had skated well in the qualifying rounds, so many people

Apolo Anton Ohno was all smiles in winning his first Olympic medal—a silver in the 1,000 meters. Australian Steven Bradbury *(center)* had glided past a four-skater pileup at the end of the race to capture the gold medal. The bronze medal went to Mathieu Turcotte *(right)* of Canada.

were convinced that this should have been his race. What many people did not know was Bradbury's own history in the sport. This was his fourth time in the Olympics, and he had put in both sweat and blood to get there, literally. In one dramatic 1994 World Cup race, Bradbury was sent airborne only to land on top of other skaters. He lost four of his body's six liters of blood from a laceration that traversed all four of his quad muscles and needed an incredible 111 stitches. And that was not the only sacrifice the Australian had made for the love of his sport. In 2000, he crashed headfirst into a barrier, breaking his neck. Here, though, Bradbury's sacrifices over the years had paid off—with luck and a time of 1 minute 29.109 seconds, he had become the first Australian to win a gold medal in the Winter Olympic Games. He told a *New York Times* journalist, "To have four [skaters] go down all at once is not something that happens. . . . I won't take the medal for a race that I won, but as a reward for the last 10 years and the effort for myself."

The Australian skater with the spiked blond hair and eyebrow piercing was surprised by the race's unpredictable conclusion, telling reporters that, as soon as he crossed the finish line, he thought to himself, "Hang on a minute, I think I just won."

Either Ohno or Jack Mortell, the leader of the U.S. short-track team, could have easily demanded a rerace, but they took the result in stride, putting their faith in the referee's decision not to order a restart within the 30-minute time limit allowed.

When it came time for the medal presentation, a smiling Ohno limped to his place at the side of the podium. The one-inch cut he suffered during the race had meant six stitches in his inner left thigh. Bradbury stood in the middle with the gold around his neck. Ohno's sideways scramble had earned him silver, and Turcotte's slide had won him bronze. Li had been disqualified. Ohno showed his usual sportsmanship toward Bradbury, his friend and bootmaker, being the first to shake the gold-medal winner's hand on the medal stand. Ohno told the media he was "really happy" for Bradbury, and of the race, he told a *New York Times* reporter, "I skated it exactly like I wanted. Unfortunately, I went down in the last corner. But this is the sport I train for. I got the silver medal, so I can't complain." Of the first of four possible medals, Ohno had won silver, and the sport of short-track speed skating had lived up to its hype—the 1,000-meter race proved that short track was anything but predictable.

SKATING THE 1,500 METERS

The day after Ohno received his stitches was the U.S. speed-skating team's optional practice day. The injured skater opted not to attend, giving himself a day of rest after the frenzied race the previous night. With only three days until his next event, Ohno had a swollen thigh and was hobbling around on crutches. Even so, he decided to bypass another course of anti-biotics and opted for alternative therapy with his physician, Dr. Lawrence Lavine. Everyone but Yuki was skeptical of this deci-sion, but by the time the 1,500-meter race was set to take place, the swelling in Ohno's thigh had gone down and there were no signs of infection. The skater knew he was good to go. This was the first time the 1,500-meter short-track event was being held at the Olympics, and despite his injury, Ohno breezed through the preliminaries.

Because of the events that had led to the 1,000-meter spec-tacle, Ohno went into the final of this race with a different plan of attack. During most of the event's 13½ laps, the skaters stuck together in a tight, unrelenting pack, but Ohno wanted breath-ing room and decided to hang back from the rest. He began to question this risky move when it became apparent to him that finding a gap large enough to make a pass might not happen. With two laps remaining, Ohno got the crowd roaring and on its feet when he made a chancy move past three skaters. He was now second only to South Korea's Kim Dong-Sung, the current World Cup champion. In the final turn, Ohno made a breakaway attempt to pass the leader on the inside, only to find himself impeded by Kim. While Ohno had made his move to charge ahead, Kim made a small, sudden shift that instinctively caused Ohno to raise his arms into the air, believing he needed to protect himself from a collision. Spectators interpreted the move as Ohno's indication that he had been impeded during his attempt to pass the South Korean. The dramatic gesture also caught the attention of race officials. The race ended with Kim

In a close-fought 1,500-meter race at the 2002 Olympics, Apolo Ohno backed off after trying to pass Kim Dong-Sung *(left)*. After the race, the officials disqualified Kim for impeding Ohno, giving the U.S. skater his first Olympic gold medal. The ruling angered the South Koreans.

skating across the finish line first. Ohno, with a time of 2 minutes 18.541 seconds, crossed over the line for a second silver medal.

As in the previous race, the crowd went wild, booing Kim's seemingly illegal move. Ohno waited breathlessly to hear the official result. He had been happy with the silver in the 1,000 meters because it had been a clean race, but this time Ohno knew that he had been the victim of an illegal move. Soon the call came in, and race officials explained what had happened on the ice. They said the South Korean's move was cross-tracking, which they defined as any move to "improperly cross the course of or in any way interfere with another competitor." Upon the officials' announcement that Kim was disqualified, Ohno sank to his knees and then gave his father a huge hug—the ruling meant Ohno had won the gold.

His South Korean opponent was not so pleased, however. While skating what he thought was his victory lap around the ice, he angrily threw down the flag of his nation that he had been carrying when he heard of the decision.

This time, the medal ceremony included bronze winner Marc Gagnon of Canada, who before his third-place finish had been the current world champion in the 1,500 meters, and silver medalist Li Jiajun, who had caused all the commotion in the 1,000 meters, resulting in his disqualification. Standing proudly at the podium's center was Ohno with his first Olympic gold medal shining brightly from around his neck. The fans' excitement was palpable. While on the podium, Ohno could feel the ground under his feet shaking with their enthusiasm—an earthquake of joy. And he could see his father—his short-track partner all these years—on the side, crying for the moment they both had waited for so long.

THE ANGER OF SOUTH KOREA

Ohno still had two chances to earn more medals, the 500-meter race and the 5,000-meter team relay. The skater, though, was more than content with his one gold. He told reporters, "I'm good now. They can just go throw me in the desert and bury me."

Unfortunately, his victory would come back to haunt him. At the time, South Korea's head coach, Jun Myung-Kyu, or "Big Jon" as he is known in the skating community, was extremely angered by the referee's call. In fact, the entire South Korean Olympic delegation was incensed by the outcome. The head of the delegation, Park Sung-in, told a South

Korean reporter, "Frankly speaking, I want to boycott the Games and go back home. I can't bear to watch any more of these unfair rulings."

The South Korean team was not alone in its feelings. The day after the 1,500-meter race and Ohno's golden win, the U.S. Olympic Committee was bombarded with threatening e-mails. Threats had actually started to come in after Ohno's silver-medal win in the 1,000-meter event. The number of e-mails was so large—16,000 in total—that the messages crashed the USOC server and kept it down for nine hours. The USOC turned over all the threatening e-mails, mostly from places and sources in South Korea, to the Federal Bureau of Investigation.

The South Koreans did not leave as Park had threatened. They did, however, file an appeal with the Court of Arbitration for Sport (CAS) and the International Olympic Committee (IOC). Coach Jun insisted that Ohno had been trailing the South Korean skater and not skating faster. Kim, he said, had impeded no one. The coach claimed that Ohno's display was overly dramatic and that the referee was not up to Olympic standards. He told all this to the media, but not to American journalists, with whom he refused to speak. Jun believed that American athletes were being shown favoritism because of media pressure. He insisted that, after the incident in the 1,000-meter race, Ohno was being portrayed as a victim of inappropriately aggressive Asian athletes. The coach's claim may have seemed outlandish to some, since Ohno himself is of Asian heritage.

Two days after the appeal was filed, the CAS met to look at the tapes of the race and to talk to the referees as well as other skaters and witnesses. The court upheld Kim's disqualification, and the IOC agreed with the ruling. Ohno's gold was now secure, but for the young Olympic medalist, the incident would prove to be only the beginning of a troublesome relationship with the nation of South Korea.

OHNO'S DEFEAT

Unfortunately, not even the high of winning gold could ward off the effects of both the flu and an upper-leg injury. When it came time to race the 500-meter preliminaries, Ohno was in rough shape. He was feeling ill, and the stitches in his thigh were causing him pain. The shorter and more intense race would require an explosive start from its participants, but Ohno just could not do it. He got off the starting line slowly and by the third lap, he found himself in third place. Ohno, though, was determined not to give up. He skated his way toward Japan's short-track threat Satoru Terao, intending to pass. What happened next isn't completely clear, but it was a sort of turnabout, since Ohno found himself in a situation similar to that of his disgruntled Korean competitor in the 1,500 meters, Kim Dong-Sung.

After the race was over, some reports said that Ohno's outside blade caught Terao; others said that Ohno knocked into his competitor while trying to make the pass. Even after viewing the tapes later himself, Ohno could not clearly see what had happened on the ice. What he does know is that he expected a collision and to protect himself, he put up his arm as a defensive maneuver. He concedes that, from some vantage points, it may have looked like an illegal push. Ohno managed to cross the finish line third, but the referees disqualified him for the move in question, giving Terao, not Ohno, a spot in the finals.

The double medalist's final chance for more Olympic glory came in the 5,000-meter team relay, an event that looked good for Team U.S.A. Ohno felt that his team had a good game plan—to get in front and stay in front. But in the predictably unpredictable spectacle that is short track, a lot of skaters took spills during the race, among them Li, Gagnon, and an Italian team member. When Ohno's teammate Rusty Smith hit a block and went down with 26 laps to go in the 45-lap race, it spelled doom for the United States. The team never recovered

(continues on page 78)

Other Notable Individuals

KRISTI YAMAGUCHI

Born on July 12, 1971, in Hayward, California, to parents who had been forcibly moved to internment camps during World War II, Kristi Yamaguchi had what is known as clubfeet. In this condition, one or both feet are twisted out of their normal position, interfering with regular movement. Kristi's condition improved when an orthopedic specialist recommended physical therapy, corrective shoes, and a special brace worn during sleep.

It was a routine trip to the mall that changed Kristi's life. While shopping, she and her mother noticed a rink set up for a special show. Kristi's eyes became transfixed on the figure skaters gliding and twirling in their bright, shiny costumes. At the age of 4, she was hooked. From that moment on, she begged her mother to let her skate, and finally, her mother conceded once Kristi entered first grade. The young girl dedicated herself to her sport, perfecting daring jumps, spins, and landings. Soon she was competing with a prowess and grace like no other.

During her skating career, Yamaguchi has had many achievements and received many honors, much like Apolo Anton Ohno. A shining moment in her life occurred during the Albertville Winter Olympics in 1992. At those Games, she became the first female figure skater to win a gold medal for the United States since her childhood idol, Dorothy Hamill, had done so in 1976.

Among the other titles Yamaguchi can claim are two-time world champion, U.S. national champion, and four-time world professional champion. The acclaimed skater was also one of the few women in the United States to compete in both individual and pairs figure skating. In 1988, she and her partner, Rudy Galindo, were the world junior pairs champions. She and Galindo won U.S. senior pairs titles the following two years.

The honors Yamaguchi has received are many. In 1996, *American Skating World* named her skater of the year. In 2005, the accomplished figure skater was inducted into the U.S. Olympic Committee Hall of Fame. And she attended the Salt Lake City Winter Olympics as the 2002 Games' official goodwill ambassador.

Over the years, skating has remained one of Yamaguchi's passions. For 10 years, from 1992 to 2002, she skated with the traveling ice show Stars on Ice alongside other skating greats like Scott Hamilton and Ekaterina Gordeeva. To make figure skating more accessible to others, she has written two books, one an autobiography titled *Kristi Yamaguchi, Always Dream*; the other, a how-to guide, *Figure Skating for Dummies*.

Yamaguchi has a few other passions as well. One is her family. In 2000, she married National Hockey League player Bret Hedican, and they now have two daughters. One project of great importance to the skating star is the Always Dream Foundation, a charity that she created in 1996 to help support organizations that work to positively influence the lives of disadvantaged kids. The name is derived from the motto that inspired Yamaguchi through many years of her life. Her foundation has provided computers for after-school mentoring programs and sponsored summer camps for children with disabilities.

Two coincidences in the lives of Yamaguchi and Ohno involve photography and dancing. A photo shoot with renowned photographer Annie Leibovitz is one thing they share. Like Ohno and his appearaance in the (PRODUCT) RED campaign for Gap, Yamaguchi was among the first celebrities Leibovitz photographed for the Got Milk? milk-mustache advertising campaign. But perhaps, most incredibly, is the fact that they each appeared on the show *Dancing with the Stars,* especially since both two-stepped and cha-cha'd their way past the competition to take home the show's top prize, a mirror ball trophy.

(continued from page 75)

the speed it needed to medal in the event. Coming in fourth, Ohno was disappointed for his teammates but quite content with his own personal victories and the silver and gold he now wore proudly around his neck.

OHNO THE CELEBRITY

The skater's performances at the Games may have been over, but his stardom was just beginning. Security at the Games, which occurred after the September 11, 2001, terrorist attacks, was incredibly tight, with guards, guns, and checkpoints all around. On their way to an interview with NBC, Yuki and Apolo were tucked inside a chauffeur-driven vehicle being inspected by soldiers for potential bombs. Despite the serious job at hand, one soldier smiled wide when he saw the Olympic short-track star sitting inside the car. He stopped momentarily to tell Ohno how proud they all were of him. Ohno was flabbergasted and flattered.

After the Games, Ohno refused to take a break—he had the 2002 World Championships in Montreal to think about. Some gold medalists choose to skip this event, but Ohno was not going to let any opportunity to skate pass him by. Strictly by chance, he aggravated an old ankle injury during training, and his doctor advised him to pull out of the World Championships to take a well-deserved and necessary break. Ohno had turned down an invitation to Sir Elton John's Oscar party in order to train, but now that he was free, he checked to see if the offer was still open. When he found out it was, he immediately phoned Dave Creswell to accompany him as a thank-you for all of his help. Ohno firmly believed that Creswell's techniques played a major role in his Olympic achievements. Starstruck together, the two hobnobbed with the likes of Halle Berry and Denzel Washington, and Ohno posed for pictures with celebrities like Harrison Ford and Ozzy and Sharon Osbourne. Ohno found it amazing that Hollywood stars were seeking him out to chat. He was now a celebrity in his own right.

The popular skater recognized by his trademark head-band and soul patch was asked to make dozens of television

After his showing at the 2002 Olympics, Apolo Anton Ohno was in demand, appearing on talk shows, at Hollywood parties, and in photo shoots. In May 2002, he rang the opening bell at the New York Stock Exchange. With him were *(from left)* Lori Roth of Nike; Richard Grasso, chairman of the stock exchange; and Apolo's father, Yuki.

appearances. On *The Tonight Show with Jay Leno,* Ohno got some good ribbing when Leno teased him about cutting himself shaving before the show. He followed up as a guest on Conan O'Brien's late-night talk show, and he was speechless

OHNO'S TRADEMARK

A soul patch is a strip of facial hair that runs from the lower lip down to the chin. Beatniks and jazz musicians popularized the look in the 1950s and 1960s. Apolo Ohno fast became known for the one he sported, and during the 2002 Salt Lake City Olympics, one could see the popular skater's almost cult-like following of both guys and girls that filled the stands. The giveaway? The patch of fake hair these fans had pasted onto their own chins.

The fakes were the brainchild of Seattle TV host John Curley, who was covering the global event for his station. He knew he wanted to show support for his hometown skater, but Curley also knew that banners and flags were hard to get through the tight security. So the day before the 1,500-meter short-track finals, Curley bought some double-stick tape and $70 worth of fake fur, apparently enough to create 3,000 imitation soul patches. The next day Curley quickly found he was only one of thousands wanting to show Ohno their love. The TV host's fellow supporters could not get enough of the fake facial hair, eagerly taking the patches off his hands and sticking them right onto their chins.

The fake patch syndrome did not stop there. After Mayor Greg Nickels of Seattle announced March 15, 2002, as Apolo Ohno Day, Washington Governor Gary Locke adhered a fake soul patch to his own chin in honor of the Olympic champion.

There is, however, a secret behind the trademark. In *People* magazine, Ohno admitted that the soul patch he so famously sports on his chin is there because it's the only place hair will grow on his face!

when Rosie O'Donnell presented him with a new car during his appearance on her program. On MTV's *TRL,* Ohno even surprised everyone by doing some break dancing for host Carson Daly.

Another perk of Ohno's newfound fame was a four-day photo shoot in the Dominican Republic with famed photographer Bruce Weber for a layout in the fashion magazine *W.* Ohno was posing on the beach with his medals around his neck when he and Weber caught wind that Bill, Hillary, and Chelsea Clinton were also there enjoying some time off together. Much to his astonishment, Ohno found himself standing alongside the former first family for a group photo, with the Clintons treating *him* like the celebrity during the quick session.

That year, Ohno was also included in *People* magazine's "50 Most Beautiful People" issue. In addition, he was honored with an invitation from the White House. There, President George W. Bush told the young man that his staff had suffered from a severe case of "Ohno-mania" during the Olympics.

Ohno took advantage of his new celebrity status on and off into 2004, but after that he returned to the basics, life in his dorm at the U.S. Olympic Training Center in Colorado Springs and his rigorous workout and training schedule. He had more work to do.

8

The Wins
Keep On Coming

The young and now world-famous skater enjoyed his celebrity status, but he also knew when it was time to return his focus to short track. In a December 2004 *Sports Illustrated* article, Apolo Anton Ohno said, "I had to tone down the celebrity thing this year. The Olympics are a year away, and I've been on a wild ride."

Ohno had by now built a reputation as a short-track skater who was hard to pass on the ice, and he had every intention of staying on top. Part of his plan involved altering his workout regimen by strength training under the wing of former kickboxer John Schaeffer, who was now a professional trainer for the likes of martial artists, boxers, and power lifters. Later, just before the 2006 Winter Olympic Games, Ohno told NBC Sports of uprooting his old routine to change everything, not just the weight training but also his nutrition program and his training on and off the ice: "It's hard to change with a sport that's always getting faster, people getting stronger, new guys are coming up, especially in my sport. I felt like I needed something to help me to be able to compete at the top level."

THE SHADOW OF SOUTH KOREA

The people of South Korea must have viewed the determined skater as a real threat on the ice. Apparently still feeling the sting a year and a half after Ohno's 2002 Olympic victory, people sent death threats via his Web site and several fan sites when he was scheduled to compete in a World Cup event in Jeonju City, South Korea. These Internet threats were compounded by a report in one Korean newspaper that Ohno was "the most hated athlete in South Korea."

Only a week before the competition, which was to take place from November 28 to 30, 2003, Ohno and the people around him decided that it would be best to err on the side of safety, and he pulled out of the World Cup event. The decision was not an easy one for the competitive-minded skater. By this point in the 2003–2004 World Cup season, he had racked up eight golds, five silvers, and two bronzes. Ohno was the skater to beat, since he held the overall title for the previous 2002–2003 World Cup season. Removing himself from competition would have a negative impact on his World Cup standing.

Ohno issued a statement to the press about the situation, "It is unfortunate that a few people feel the need to make death threats against me. I am an athlete, not a politician." Despite losing this opportunity to score points that would contribute to his overall standing for the World Cup season, Ohno upheld his reputation as a tough competitor and placed third overall for the 2003–2004 season.

The specter of South Korea kept Ohno from another important short-track event in March 2005, the world team championships in Chuncheon, South Korea. By the fall of 2005, however, the need to compete trumped risk. During an

Olympic year, the International Skating Union schedules only four short-track World Cup events, rather than six. With the next Olympic Games less than five months away, Ohno knew he could not afford to lose an opportunity to measure his own skating and that of his top competitors.

This time around Ohno felt a bit more secure in his decision. Many Korean officials and the Korean Skating Union all ensured his safety, and no death threats had been communicated. He also had the comfort of comments from fellow

South Korean riot police stood guard in October 2005 to protect Apolo Anton Ohno from protesters at Incheon International Airport near Seoul. After his victory in the 1,500 meters at the 2002 Olympics, Ohno had been the subject of threats from some South Koreans and had stayed away from two previous competitions in the country.

skaters, South Koreans themselves. At various competitions, several had sought out Ohno to tell him that he did indeed have fans in their country. In an interview with *Men's Journal*, one of the world's top skaters at the time, South Korean Ahn Hyun-Soo, spoke highly of his competitor, "Even though some Koreans have bad feelings about Apolo, the world is learning from him. He is a master."

Korean officials made good on their word to keep the 23-year-old star safe. When Ohno arrived at the Seoul airport for the World Cup, he was greeted by 100 police officers in riot gear, all there for his protection. At the event itself, Ohno proved that even distractions about his personal safety could not keep him from dominating the ice. He skated to wins in the 1,000- and 3,000-meter finals.

Upon returning from his first trip to South Korea since the Olympic upset in 2002, Ohno spoke to reporters about the resentment that had kept him from the nation for so long. "It was just some people manifesting this image of me and anti-American sentiment," he said. "I was really bothered by it. I grew up around Asian cultures. I have a lot of friends who are Korean. I couldn't understand it." With his appearance and victories in Seoul behind him, Ohno could now place full concentration on the Olympics.

ANOTHER ROUND OF OLYMPIC TRIALS

For all the skaters at the Olympic Trials, short track once again proved its reputation as a rough-and-tumble sport. During the 500-meter finals, Ohno was pushed from behind, a collision on the ice that caused him to falter, but fortunately, not to fall. Just as he recovered his balance from this hard knock, another near-collision broke his stride. First place was out of his grasp, but he skated across the finish line for second place.

Crazy moves were the name of the game in these trials. *The New York Times* quoted Ohno as saying, "I'm just trying to stay out of trouble. There's a lot of fighting going on out there. It's dangerous, no matter where you are, in the front, back, middle." In the 1,000 meters, Ohno was skating close to the pack, but with four laps to go, he pulled a seamless

Being Asian American
INDUCTION INTO THE ASIAN HALL OF FAME

As a single father, alone in the United States, with any family to help him with childrearing thousands of miles away, Yuki Ohno did his best to raise his son right. When he saw the potential for his child to go astray, he got Apolo into activities like swimming and inline skating to keep him occupied. The pair took Apolo's involvement in sports quite seriously, and when the boy's natural talent for short-track skating became apparent, they dedicated themselves to Apolo's success.

The father and son's mostly harmonious relationship erupted when Apolo refused to get on a plane to go to training in Lake Placid, New York. Although the situation resolved itself and Apolo eventually went to Lake Placid—a crucial stop in his short-track destiny—he remained furious at his father for quite some time. Upon reflection, though, the stubborn skater has stated that his father did, indeed, know what was best for his son. "He comes from that Asian background; he's strict," Apolo said. This strictness and insistence that Apolo make a choice for his future paid off abundantly when he took home five medals in two Olympic Games. Like other Asian-American skating Olympians who paved the way before him, such as Michelle Kwan and Kristi Yamaguchi, Ohno became a sports sensation and a role model for others around the world.

In recognition of his contributions to the Asian-American community, Ohno was inducted into the Asian Hall of Fame in April 2007, joining an auspicious list of honorees. The Hall of Fame was created in 2004 by Robert Chinn, founder of Seattle's United States Savings and Loan Bank—the first bank in the United States owned breakaway move as they all rounded the corner. In almost the blink of an eye, Ohno had gained a lead of a quarter lap over his nearest competitor. He sailed easily to a first-place finish.

by an Asian American. Asian Hall of Fame inductees over the years have included former Washington Governor Gary Locke, painter and sculptor George Tsutakawa, painter Z.Z. Wei, and actor Yuji Okumoto. Business executive and attorney Loida Nicolas Lewis, who was born in the Philippines and was the first Asian woman to pass the New York State Bar Exam, was inducted alongside Ohno that spring.

The honor came during Ohno's stint on *Dancing with the Stars.* Always one to take his work seriously, Ohno was joined on his trip from Los Angeles to Seattle by his *Dancing* co-star, Julianne Hough, as well as by strength and conditioning coach and nutritionist John Schaeffer, so the skating star could keep practicing and stay on track physically and nutritionally. The induction ceremony was held at the Asian Resource Center in Seattle's Chinatown/International District, where Ohno arrived via a Rolls-Royce. With his father looking on from the audience, Ohno told those gathered that he was humbled by the honor. He paid tribute to his father and remarked, "My life has always been about hard work, dedication, and sacrifice." Ohno's framed likeness will adorn the walls of the Asian Hall of Fame, inspiring others to work hard, to dream, and to achieve.

In an interview with *NWA WorldTraveler* magazine, Ohno spoke of the pride he has not only in his Japanese roots but in his country as well. "I'm very proud of my father's Japanese heritage, but I'm also very proud to be American." For all his contributions, America, no doubt, is equally proud to have Ohno.

The 1,500-meter event was a different story altogether. For most of the race, Ohno had U.S. skaters Alex Izykowski and J.P. Kepka following close on his tail. He could not shake them and pull ahead. That is, until the two skaters collided, taking each other out of the race. Again, Ohno skated his way to first and a certain spot on the U.S. Olympic Team.

THE 2006 OLYMPIC GAMES

Ohno went into the 2006 Olympic Games in Turin, Italy, that February with a lot of enthusiasm. He was excited about the chance to compete on the Olympic stage again and was also hoping that his sport would garner even more attention than it had in 2002. As always, Ohno went into the Games focused. But the usually solitary skater was not alone. This time he was accompanied by his girlfriend of two years, Allison Baver, a short-track skater for the U.S. Women's Team and a former cheerleader from Sinking Spring, Pennsylvania. At 25, she was two years older than her boyfriend, but like him, she was at the top of the U.S. team's roster. Her forte was the 500 meters and 1,500 meters, so people were expecting medals for her in both events. Given both athletes' competitive nature, the races the two had scheduled for the day after Valentine's Day would mean little time for romance in old Italy. Baver told reporters, "It's part of his personality. . . . He's not concerned about any-thing else except training, competing."

By the time the 2006 Winter Olympics approached, most of the Apolo Ohno–South Korea controversy had died down. But with South Korean skater Ahn Hyun-Soo—a three-time world champ and one of the skaters knocked out of the 1,000 meters in 2002—pegged as Ohno's toughest competition at the Games, a rivalry still flourished. Once again, the media and enthusiastic fans had high expectations for Ohno, but he had a much cooler attitude about the Games ahead. He told *Sports Illustrated*, "One goal was just to get to Torino.

Now I just want to finish and say, 'I did my best,' regardless of the outcome. That would be perfect." Although these Games would prove to be a bit bumpy, Ohno would eventually experience more perfection than he ever could have hoped for.

THE 1,500-METER DEBACLE

During the two weeks of the Games, Ohno was scheduled to hit the ice every three days. His first event on Sunday, February 12, had him defending his controversial 1,500-meter title from 2002. In his qualifying heat, Ohno made winning the 13½-lap race look easy. The top two skaters of the next race, the semifinal, would move on to the final, but the semifinal played out differently from Ohno's qualifying heat. Ohno was behind race leader Li Ye of China. Ohno refused to just hang back. Instead, he tried to overtake Li in the curve before the final lap. As if locked in a bumper-car cage, the two collided and Ohno's left hand became tangled with Li's skates. Ohno lost his balance and his momentum, and although he managed to regain his composure, he also lost his second-place spot, finishing fourth out of six. Ohno was shut out of the finals and his first shot at gold in Turin. The skaters who made it to the podium were China's Li Jiajun with bronze, South Korean Lee Ho-Suk with silver, and Ohno's toughest rival, Ahn, with gold.

Fans and teammates were obviously disappointed that Ohno did not make the finals, but most knew that with short track, such occurrences were par for the course. Among the disappointed was Ohno's girlfriend, Baver, who told *The New York Times,* "It really breaks my heart to see. Because I know he's the best skater in the world."

MOVING ON TO THE 1,000 METERS

On Wednesday, February 15, Ohno seemed back in form and unwilling to take any more chances. While on the ice in his initial heat of the 1,000-meter race, he kept safely to the back, waiting to charge ahead only in the final lap. The strategy worked, and he won this heat to advance to the quarterfinals, set for Saturday, February 18. Wednesday also brought hope for Team U.S.A. when Ohno and his teammates finished the 5,000-meter relay semifinals with the fastest time. The U.S. relay team could look forward to going for gold in the finals on Saturday, February 25, the second-to-last day of the Games.

Ohno's usual MO during any competition is to isolate himself and maintain his focus, but during the Olympic Games, he tried something different: being a little more social. He took to the computer to read e-mail, enjoyed chats with friends and

After the 1,000-meter race at the 2006 Olympics, bronze medalist Apolo Ohno congratulated the winner, Ahn Hyun-Soo of South Korea. Ahn's countryman, Lee Ho-Suk (left), had taken the silver medal.

relatives, and even listened to advice that others had to give, like the e-mail that read, "Here and now, breathe and relax," a statement that friend Dave Creswell would have probably agreed with wholeheartedly.

On Saturday, February 18, Ohno raced his way successfully into the finals of the 1,000 meters. Ohno got off to a good start in the final, skating well, but in the last lap, he could not get past the two South Koreans in the lead, Ahn and Lee. The Koreans repeated their 1-2 finish, and Ohno happily took bronze, his first medal of the Games. For him, bronze was no disappointment and at the flower ceremony following the race, Ohno had nothing but waves and smiles for the cheering crowd.

So far, the South Koreans were clearly dominating these Games, and the media were curious about their lingering rivalry with Ohno. In a press conference after the race, Ahn was asked about Ohno's gold-medal win back in 2002. Just as Ahn was about to answer, Ohno walked in and gave Ahn two congratulatory pats on the back on the way to his chair. In essence the question had been answered; any hard feelings over those events four years ago had been erased.

Ahn did admit that it felt pretty good to get the better of such an acclaimed short-track skater: "This time, from the very first preliminary race, I competed against Ohno and I won every time. And that really gives me a special feeling." In return, Ohno told journalists that the Koreans had a long history of strong skaters and that "for him [Ahn] to add another medal to his collection is very, very impressive. They skated very well tonight."

A PERFECT RACE

Next on the line for Ohno was the 500 meters, which came the following Saturday. For Ahn, a first-place finish would mean a gold-medal trifecta in the men's individual short-track events. In his semifinal, Ohno was good for only a third-place showing, and only the top two skaters could advance to the finals. But Li Jiajun was disqualified for impeding Ohno, and Ohno took Li's spot in the finals. Given Ohno's default into the finals, no one could have predicted what happened next.

The first two attempts to get the 500-meter final going ended in false starts by other skaters. When the starting gun went off the third time, Ohno moved off the line in a flash, so fast that one might have expected to see flames burning up the ice behind him. Not often in short track, not even in its shortest race, does one skater break away so quickly that no one is left to challenge his or her lead. Ahn, a third gold on his mind, tried desperately to catch up, attempting to pass the two Canadians between him and Ohno. He managed to get around Eric Bedard, but he could not make it past François-Louis Tremblay. When the 23-year-old from Seattle skated across the finish, he looked back over his shoulder, raised his arms in the air, and gave out a shout of joy. He had won gold in a clean race with no collisions or impacts to cause contro-versy. The *Philadelphia Inquirer* quoted an elated Ohno, "I couldn't believe it. There was so much emotion and so much passion that went through my body, it was crazy. . . . I've been searching my entire career for the perfect race, and that was it." Indeed, it had been a perfect race, and the two-time gold medalist had second-place finisher Tremblay to back him up. "I was waiting for one mistake, and he didn't do one," the Canadian told reporters.

Ahn was a little less congenial after the race. Ohno had finished in 41.935 seconds, Tremblay in 42.002, and Ahn in 42.089. Ahn had only been .154 seconds away from a gold sweep in the individual short-track events. That may have col-ored his thoughts on the results. Once the South Korean saw the race in replays, he wondered if Ohno's incredible start had instead been yet another false one. Although Ahn seemed dis-enchanted, he said he would not contest the referee's decision

Apolo Anton Ohno shouted for joy as he crossed the finish line in first place in the 500-meter race at the 2006 Olympics. Ohno led the race from start to finish. He said, "I've been searching my entire career for the perfect race, and that was it."

that this had been nothing but a good, clean race. For Ohno, the win remained nothing but perfection.

ONE LAST MEDAL

Ohno had little time to rest on the laurels of his breathtaking race; only 32 minutes after his golden finish, he was ready to compete in the men's 5,000-meter relay. Although Ohno made a crucial move past one of Italy's skaters during his session of laps on the rink, the U.S. team failed to place first as hoped. Instead, the South Korean team once again proved its short-track prowess, taking the gold. Canada earned the silver, and the U.S. team, composed of Ohno, Rusty Smith, Alex Izykowski, and J.P. Kepka, took the bronze. Smith spoke of the U.S. effort, "I knew we'd get bronze with about two laps to go when Apolo slowed down to set them [the Italian team] up. I knew we'd be all right."

By the end of the Turin Olympics, Ohno was the holder of five Olympic medals—two from 2002 and three from these Winter Games. He was now tied for a record with one of his speed-skating idols, Eric Heiden, a long-track skater who at the age of 21 in 1980 at Lake Placid, New York, did what no other Olympic athlete had done before—win five individual gold medals in a single Olympics. Ohno and Heiden were now the only two American men who could claim a total of five Winter Olympic medals.

9

The Bright Future of a Bright Star

After his three-medal haul in Turin, Apolo Anton Ohno took almost a year off from international competition. But his performance at the World Short Track Speedskating Championships in Milan in March 2007 showed that the time away for Ohno did not seem to be of any consequence as he won the 1,500 meters. Eight days after the world championships, he gave something entirely new a shot.

DANCING BACK INTO THE LIMELIGHT

On March 19, 2007, Ohno made his debut on the fourth season of the show *Dancing with the Stars,* a celebrity dance competition. He joined a group of other celebrities that included model Paulina Porizkova, country singer and *Hannah Montana* father Billy Ray Cyrus, entertainment reporter Leeza Gibbons, and boxer Laila Ali, the daughter of Ohno's boyhood hero Muhammad Ali. On the show, each celebrity is paired with a professional ballroom dancer. Ohno was teamed up with a newcomer to the show, 18-year-old Julianne Hough.

The show requires a lot of training, practice, and stamina—all things Ohno was familiar with, and during his 10 weeks on the show, Ohno found the schedule just as grueling as that of short track. Even though he was taking a break from the ice, his trainers compelled him to keep up his workout routine while doing the show. Ohno said his days became repetitions of eat, train, rehearse; eat, train, rehearse. Each day for the dancer/skater started at 5:30 A.M. He would spend four to six hours training for the show with another two to three hours of off-ice workout time. His usual eight hours of sleep was sometimes down to three.

Ohno and his dance partner found that they had a lot in common. Both had left home at an early age to pursue their careers. Hough, a Salt Lake City native, began to dance at age 3 and moved to London at age 10 to train and dance competitively. Like Ohno, she joined the world-class rank of her profession, becoming a two-time Latin dance world champion. Hough said that their shared focus translated onto the dance floor. During training and rehearsals, she added, he was more than attentive and really listened to her instructions.

One of the biggest difficulties the skater had to overcome as a new dancer was his posture. Ohno told *People Weekly*, "I've molded my body into this shape for the past 12 years of my life." Ballroom dancing required him to forget the hunch and constant left turns he does while skating and instead stand straight and move gracefully to the right. Ohno soon learned another difference between dance and short track. He discovered that dancing was judged on more than just its quality or technical performance; there was also a "wow" factor involved, a connection with the audience through the dancers' moves on the floor.

Ohno and Hough performed well throughout the season and were the first pair to receive a perfect score of 30 from the show's often rigorous judges. They remained in the top three

Dancing with the Stars contestants Apolo Anton Ohno and Julianne Hough danced the tango in May 2007 during a concert sponsored by a California radio station. Ohno brought the same drive and focus to *Dancing with the Stars* that he brings to short-track skating.

over the continuing weeks. The season finale had Ohno and Hough stepping out against Joey Fatone, a former member of the boy band 'NSYNC and his partner, Kym Johnson, as well as Laila Ali and her partner, Maksim Chmerkovskiy, who came into that night's competition in third place. Over the course of the night, Fatone, who later described Ohno as a "solid competitor," and Johnson danced a *Star Wars*-inspired tango; Ali and Chmerkovskiy tore up the floor with the mambo, while Ohno and Hough stepped their way through the paso doble. Both Ohno and Fatone earned perfect scores of 60 out of 60, but the clincher for Ohno and Hough came with the tabulation of the viewing public's vote. *Dancing*'s final scoring system combines half the judges' score with half the popular vote. The short-track star paralleled his skating life with a win of the show's mirror ball trophy, and to make the victory even sweeter, it happened on his twenty-fifth birthday, May 22. Ohno said it was his best birthday ever.

Of the Olympian's dance win, judge Carrie Ann Inaba told *People* magazine, "I'm so excited to see Apolo win. He took it so seriously. He truly mastered the dances. He was the best technical dancer. Apolo and Julianne brought a whole new energy to the dance floor. You never knew quite what they were going to do."

The experience was a happy one for Ohno. He said that he had made many good friends and that he had gotten to come out of his shell a little bit—the show let people see him as more than just the intense short-track athlete. After the show, Ohno said he was recognized on the street as "that dancer guy," not as an Olympic hero.

A RETURN TO THE ICE

Ohno's second break from skating lasted nine months. He noted that his time off was the equivalent of two full summer vacations, which in his sport was not the greatest idea. Given the experiences he had over that time, however, he was more than content with his decision.

In late December 2007, Ohno returned to the ice full time, beginning with the U.S. Short Track Championships in Utah, the new headquarters of U.S. Speedskating. Utah was also where Ohno had recently bought a home for himself. Ohno's time away from his sport seemed to have had little effect. During the 1,500-meter race, with only two laps to go, he used his now trademark move of coming from behind to capture an easy win. With a time of 2:17.725, he had earned himself yet another gold.

Ohno continued to compete both nationally and internationally, racking up more victories along the way. At the 2007 World Championships he won bronze overall and the following year captured his first overall gold in the World Championships. Then in late December 2008, he won an amazing tenth national title at the U.S. Short Track Championships.

OHNO'S CAREER HIGHLIGHTS

Following are some of Apolo Anton Ohno's achievements in short-track speed skating:

Olympic Games
2010, Bronze 1,000 meters
2010, Silver 1,500 meters
2010, Bronze 5,000-meter relay
2006, Gold 500 meters
2006, Bronze 1,000 meters
2006, Bronze 5,000-meter relay
2002, Gold 1,500 meters
2002, Silver 1,000 meters

World Cups
2004–2005, Overall Champion
2002–2003, Overall Champion
2000–2001, Overall Champion

World Championships
2008, Gold Overall
2007, Bronze Overall
2006, Bronze Overall
2005, Silver Overall
2004, Ninth Overall
2003, Fourth Overall
2001, Silver Overall
2000, Ninth Overall
1999, Fourth Overall

Junior World Championships
1999, Overall Champion

Besides buying a new home in Utah, other aspects of Ohno's life were changing as well. Shortly before his on-ice comeback, he started to train under a new coach, Jae Su Chun. Chun was hired in the spring of 2007 to lead the short-track program for U.S. Speedskating. The new coach told Ohno that his competitors were learning from him—studying and copying his moves on the ice. To keep him ahead of the pack, Chun began to teach Ohno—whom he has called the hardest-working and most focused skater he has ever seen—to change the way he skates, right down to the fundamentals. And with Ohno's ever-increasing list of wins, the tactic seems to be working.

VANCOUVER 2010

After his medal-earning performances in Turin, Italy, Ohno considered retiring from the sport of short track. But because the 2010 Olympics were to be held in Vancouver, Cananda, where he began his short-track training, he felt that his participation there would bring his career full circle.

In his first event, the 1,500-meter race, Ohno stumbled early, allowing three South Koreans to pull ahead of him. As they headed down the last turn, with Ohno in fourth place, South Korean Lee Ho-Suk made one last effort to move into first place and crashed into his teammate, Sung Si-Bak. The two skaters fell and crashed into a barrier and Ohno automatically moved into second place. A few moments later, Ohno crossed the finish line and won the silver medal.

Several days later, Ohno won his seventh medal, a bronze in the 1,000-meter race. His next event, the 500 meters, resulted in a disqualification, but Ohno bounced back and returned almost an hour later to compete in the 5,000-meter relay. After an exciting, 45-lap race, Ohno and his teammates won the bronze—his eighth medal, making him the most decorated U.S. Winter Olympian of all time.

Apolo Anton Ohno celebrated on the winner's podium at the 2008 World Championships in Gangneung, South Korea, where he won his first overall gold at the World Championships. Ohno plans to compete through the 2010 Winter Olympics in Vancouver, British Columbia.

OHNO'S HOPES AND ASPIRATIONS

When talking about his ambitions outside of short track, Ohno mentions possibilities like motivational speaking or coaching, which might be a natural course for an athlete of his abilities. Just as his sport of short track is unpredictable, some of Ohno's career considerations might seem equally unpredictable—for example, when he mentions the possibility of becoming a computer programmer.

Ohno has already had his entrée into reality TV with *Dancing,* and he has speculated with a bit of humor that perhaps he should do more reality TV following his skating career, noting that skating has all the ingredients of reality television—sacrifice, heartbreak, and drama. During the 2007 Indianapolis 500, Ohno had the opportunity to drive the pace car, which influenced another career option he talks about—auto racing, which like short track has the thrill of speed. When skating is over, there is one sure thing. Ohno says he will return to Seattle, the one place he has always considered home.

Through strength of will and a lot of hard work, Ohno made short-track history and became a part of America's own history. In fact, his skates—the ones he wore in the 2002 Salt Lake City Olympics—sit alongside other national treasures like Dorothy's ruby slippers from *The Wizard of Oz* and his long-time hero Muhammad Ali's boxing gloves as part of a popular-culture exhibit in the Smithsonian Institution National Museum of American History. No doubt whatever this superstar of skating chooses for his future, once he sets his mind to it, he will find his way straight to the top.

CHRONOLOGY

1982 Apolo Anton Ohno is born on May 22 to father Yuki Ohno and mother Jerrie Lee in Seattle, Washington.

1983 Jerrie Lee abandons Apolo and Yuki, leaving Yuki to raise his son alone.

1994 Apolo sits down with his father to watch the Winter Olympic Games in Lillehammer, Norway. He is captivated by the relatively new Olympic sport of short-track speed skating.

1996 *January* The novice skater competes in the Junior World Championship trials, ranking fourth overall.

July Apolo begins to train at the Olympic Training Center in Lake Placid, New York. He reluctantly starts the program six weeks late—he did not want to move away from home.

1997 *March* At age 14, Apolo wins the overall title at the Senior World Trials and earns himself a place on the U.S. Senior World Team.

Spring He travels to Nagano, Japan, for his first World Championships. The experience is a huge disappointment when he places 19th. It leads him to take a break from skating.

1998 *January* Apolo fails to make the Olympic team during the Olympic Trials. His father drops him off at their cabin so he can decide about his future.

February After deciding he wants to continue skating, Apolo returns to Lake Placid to train.

November Apolo places first in the 1,000 meters at an event in Hungary; it is his first World Cup victory.

1999 At the Junior World Championships, Apolo takes the Junior World Title, setting the record as the youngest skater ever to do so.

At the World Team Championships in St. Louis, Missouri, Apolo has a fateful spill on the ice that will have serious repercussions for the health of his back.

2001 *May* Apolo's back spasms are so bad that he cannot even get through an entire practice. He is diagnosed with facet syndrome.

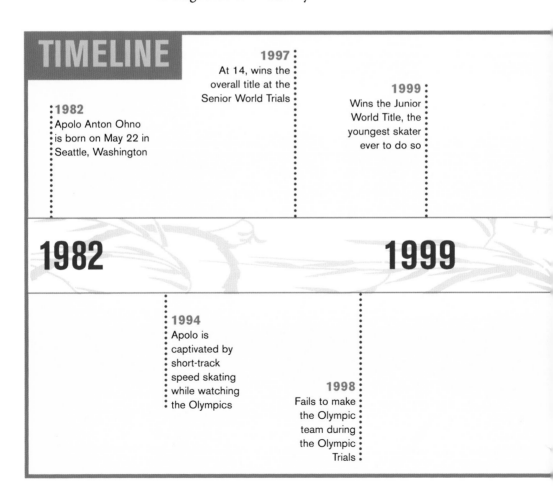

TIMELINE

1997
At 14, wins the overall title at the Senior World Trials

1982
Apolo Anton Ohno is born on May 22 in Seattle, Washington

1999
Wins the Junior World Title, the youngest skater ever to do so

1982

1999

1994
Apolo is captivated by short-track speed skating while watching the Olympics

1998
Fails to make the Olympic team during the Olympic Trials

October After some time off to recover from his back injury, Apolo participates in a World Cup event in Calgary, Alberta, Canada.

December Apolo earns a spot on the U.S. team during the Olympic Trials.

2002 *January* Ohno, Davis, and Smith are cleared of any wrongdoing in the race-fixing controversy.

February Ohno wins two medals—one silver, one gold—in the Winter Olympics in Salt Lake City, Utah. South Korea files a complaint after skater Kim Dong-Sung is disqualified, resulting

2002
Wins two medals at the Winter Olympics

2006
Wins three medals at the Winter Olympics

2010
Wins three medals at the 2010 Vancouver Olympics and becomes the most decorated U.S. Winter Olympian in history.

2002

2010

2003
Pulls out of a World Cup event in South Korea because of death threats

2007
Wins *Dancing with the Stars* competition

in Ohno's gold-medal win in the 1,500-meter event. Both the Court of Arbitration for Sport and the International Olympic Committee uphold Kim's disqualification.

2003 *November* Ohno decides to pull out of a World Cup event in South Korea because of death threats—the result of lingering anger over his 2002 Olympic victory over Kim Dong-Sung.

2005 *October* Ohno makes his first appearance in South Korea since his 2002 Olympic victory. He wins the 1,000- and 3,000-meter events at the World Cup competition.
December Ohno again earns a spot on the U.S. Olympic Team.

2006 *February* Ohno skates off with three more medals—two bronze and one gold—at the Winter Olympics in Turin, Italy.

2007 *April* Ohno is inducted into the Asian Hall of Fame in Seattle.
May After 10 weeks of competing on the series *Dancing with the Stars,* Ohno and his dance partner, Julianne Hough, win the show's top prize.
December Ohno returns to the ice full time, beginning with the U.S. Short Track Championships in Utah, where he captures gold in the 1,500 meters.

2008 *December* Ohno wins an astonishing 10th national title at the U.S. Short Track Championships.

2010 Ohno wins three medals at the 2010 Vancouver Olympics and becomes the most decorated U.S. Winter Olympian in history.

GLOSSARY

antibiotic—Medication used in the prevention and treatment of infectious diseases.

bender—A special tool skaters use to help get the minute bend in their blades just right.

blocks—Track markers along the curves of the short-track ice.

creatine—A compound the body makes and uses to store energy. Athletes use a synthetic version to increase muscle mass and improve performance.

cross-tracking—An illegal short-track maneuver in which one skater moves abruptly to cut off another skater.

dry-land workouts—Exercises and training routines that take place off the ice and are designed to improve a skater's strength, agility, coordination, balance, and speed.

facet syndrome—A painful condition in which joints in the back of the spine degenerate.

interval training—Athletic training that alternates between two or more different activities, such as running and walking, or between rates of speed or intensity.

Issei—The generation of people born in Japan who later emigrated to another country.

Nisei—The generation of people born outside of Japan to at least one Issei or non-immigrant parent.

radius gauge—A special instrument skaters use to measure amounts up to 1/1,000th of an inch in order to find flaws in the bend of their skate blades.

resistance training—Any exercise that uses external resistance, like dumbbells, to cause certain muscles to contract.

team skating—An illegal skating tactic in which an entire team works together in a way that allows a specified member to win the race.

BIBLIOGRAPHY

"Apolo Anton Ohno." *Biography Resource Center Online.* Gale Group, 2002. Reproduced in Biography Resource Center. Farmington Hills, Mich.: Gale, 2008.

"Apolo Anton Ohno: Biography." TV Guide.com. Available online. URL: http://www.tvguide.com/celebrities/apolo-anton-ohno/bio/221219.

"Apolo Anton Ohno: The Official Site." Available online. URL: http://www.apoloantonohno.com.

"Apolo Ohno: Next Asian American Olympic Hero?" *GoldSea Asian Air.* Available online. URL: http://www.goldsea.com/Air/Issues/Ohno/ohno.html.

"Apolo Ohno." *People Weekly.* May 13, 2002, p. 99.

Araton, Harvey. "Olympics: Short-Track Speed Skating; This Time, Foul Gives Ohno the Gold." *The New York Times.* February 21, 2002. Available online. URL: http://www.nytimes.com/2002/02/21/sports/olympics-short-track-speedskating-this-time-foul-gives-ohno-the-gold.html.

———. "Sports of the Times; Short-Track Skating Crashes Into View." *The New York Times.* February 18, 2002. Available online. URL: http://www.nytimes.com/2002/02/18/sports/sports-of-the-times-short-track-skating-crashes-into-view.html.

"Asian Hall of Fame" Web site. Available online. URL: http://www.asianhalloffame.org/home.htm.

Associated Press. "No Break for Ohno, Baver on Valentine's Day." NBC Sports. February 8, 2006. Available online. URL: http://nbcsports.msnbc.com/id/11239042.

———. "Ohno, Cheek to Grace Wheaties Boxes." NBC Sports. March 1, 2006. Available online. URL: http://nbcsports.msnbc.com/id/11622541.

———. "Ohno, Reutter Win National Speedskating Titles." *USA Today.* December 21, 2008. Available online. URL: http://www.usatoday.com/sports/olympics/2008-12-21-511561931_x.htm.

———. "South Korean DQ'd; Officials Promise Protest." ESPN. com. February 23, 2002. Available online. URL: http://sports. espn.go.com/oly/winter02/speed/news?id=1337596.

———. "USOC Turns Over E-Mails to FBI." ESPN.com. February 23, 2002. Available online. URL: http://sports.espn. go.com/oly/winter02/speed/news?id=1338011.

The Biography Channel. "Apolo Anton Ohno Biography." Biography.com. Available online. URL: http://www. biography.com/search/article.do?id=226021.

Cazeneuve, Brian. "Apolo Anton Ohno: Speedskater." *Sports Illustrated.* February 13, 2006, p. 45.

———. "Still on the Fast Track." *Sports Illustrated.* December 13, 2004, p. Z1.

Collie, Ashley Jude. "Need for Speed." *NWA WorldTraveler.* October 2007, pp. 54–59, 91–92. Available online. URL: http://apoloantonohno.com/articles/NWAarticle07.pdf.

Comtex News Network. "Ohno Pulls Out of World Cup Due to Death Threats." *Xinhua News Agency.* November 23, 2003.

Cosgrove, Ellen. "Apolo Ohno: America's Best Short-Track Speed Skater Makes His Olympic Debut at Age 19." *Sports Illustrated for Kids.* February 1, 2002, p. 56.

Crouse, Karen. "Ohno Captures Gold and Helps Brighten Games for the U.S." *The New York Times.* February 26, 2006. Available online. URL: http://www.nytimes.com/2006/02/26/ sports/olympics/26short.html.

———. "Ohno Hoping for Victories, and Thaw in Icy Relations with South Koreans." *The New York Times.* February 12, 2006. Available online. URL: http://www.nytimes.com/2006/02/12/ sports/olympics/12ohno.html.

———. "Ohno Sees One Slip Away." *The New York Times.* February 13, 2006. Available online. URL: http://www.nytimes. com/2006/02/13/sports/olympics/13short.html.

Davila, Florangela. "Asian Hall of Fame Inducts Olympian Ohno." *Seattle Times.* April 27, 2007. Available online. URL: http:// seattletimes.nwsource.com/html/othersports/2003683154_ ohno27.html.

Duenwald, Mary. "American Gold." *Teen People.* February 1, 2002, p.82+.

Eligon, John. "No Fuss or Hard Feelings as Ohno Fades to 3rd." *The New York Times.* February 19, 2006. Available online. URL: http://www.nytimes.com/2006/02/19/sports/olympics/19short.html.

———. "Ohno Puts Fall in Past and Moves Closer to Medals." *The New York Times.* February 16, 2006. Available online. URL: http://www.nytimes.com/2006/02/16/sports/olympics/16track.html.

Fitzpatrick, Frank. "Ohno's Goal: 'I Want to Grab Some Medals.'" *The Philadelphia Inquirer.* February 7, 2006.

Ford, Bob. "Apolo Anton Ohno Was Searching for the Perfect Race and This Was It." *The Philadelphia Inquirer.* February 25, 2006.

"Gap (PRODUCT) RED Collection Designed to Make a Difference for Africa." Press Release. Gap Inc. October 9, 2006. Available online. URL: http://www.gapinc.com/public/Media/Press_Releases/med_pr_GapProductRed100906.shtml.

Hasday, Judy L. *Kristi Yamaguchi* (Asian Americans of Achievement). New York: Chelsea House Publishers, 2007.

"History of Short Track Speed Skating." World Short Track Web site. Available online. URL: http://www.worldshorttrack.com/shorttrack/history.asp.

"In & Around Town: Asian Hall of Fame." *International Examiner.* Vol. 34, No. 09. Available online. URL: http://www.iexaminer.org/archives/?p=625.

Jones, Chris. "One Thing Perfectly: Catching Up with Apolo Ohno." *Esquire.* February 2006, p. 72+.

Judd, Ron. "Spotlight Beckons Again for Ohno." *The Seattle Times.* February 9, 2006. Available online. URL: http://seattletimes.nwsource.com/html/olympics/2002792704_olyohno09.html.

Lang, Thomas. *Going for the Gold: Apolo Anton Ohno.* New York: Avon Books, 2002.

Lewis, Michael C. "Speedskating: Ohno Poised for Return to Racing." *The Salt Lake Tribune.* December 18, 2007. Sports Section.

———. "U.S. Short-Track Championships: Ohno Wins Race After Long Layoff." *The Salt Lake Tribune.* December 22, 2007. Sports Section.

McDaniel, Melissa. *Japanese Americans* (Our Cultural Heritage). Chanhassen, Minn.: The Child's World, 2003.

Michaelis, Vicki. "Speedskater Ohno Faces Old Ghosts." *USA Today.* September 22, 2005, p. 03C.

———. "Speedskating Icon Ohno Aims to Dance into 2010 Games." *USA Today.* October 22, 2008. Available online. URL: http://www.usatoday.com/sports/olympics/2008-10-22-ohno-2010_N.htm.

Nudd, Tim. "Apolo Ohno Set to Return to Competitive Skating." People.com. December 18, 2007. Available online. URL: http://www.people.com/people/article/0,,20166911,00.html.

The Official Kristi Yamaguchi Web site. Available online. URL: http://kristiyamaguchi.com.

Ohno, Apolo Anton, with Nancy Ann Richardson. *A Journey: The Autobiography of Apolo Anton Ohno.* New York: Simon & Schuster Books for Young Readers, 2002.

"Ohno Content With 2 Medals." *The New York Times.* February 25, 2002. Available online. URL: http://www.nytimes.com/2002/02/25/sports/olympics-ohno-content-with-2-medals.html.

Orecklin, Michelle. "You Never Know Who You'll Meet." *People.* June 10, 2002, p. 75.

Peters, Jennifer L. "Blazing Blades: He Was Headed the Wrong Way; Then His Blades Helped to Steer Him Right." *Know Your World Extra.* April 26, 2002, p. 2+.

Price, S.L. "Launch of Apolo." *Sports Illustrated.* February 4, 2002, p. 122+.

———. "Speed Thrills." *Sports Illustrated.* February 25, 2002, p. 46+.

Rizzo, Monica. "Ohno A-Go-Go." *People.* April 30, 2007, pp. 87–88.

Rizzo, Monica, and Michelle Tan. "Apolo Anton Ohno Wins Dancing with the Stars." People.com. May 23, 2007.

Robbins, Liz. "Ohno Expresses No Bitterness." *The New York Times.* February 18, 2002. Available online. URL: http://query.nytimes.com/gst/fullpage.html?res=9D01EEDA1E3FF93BA25751C0A9649C8B63.

———. "Ohno Slides to Silver After Wild Collision Near Finish." *The New York Times.* February 17, 2002. Available online.

URL: http://query.nytimes.com/gst/fullpage.html?res=990D
EFDB113FF934A25751C0A9649C8B63&scp=1&sq=short-
track%20ohno%20slides%20wild%20collision&st=cse.

Roberts, Selena. "A Crisis Is Averted, but the Road Ahead Is
Still Slick." *The New York Times.* February 3, 2002. Available
online. URL: http://query.nytimes.com/gst/fullpage.html?res
=9D06E5DA123DF930A35751C0A9649C8B63&scp=1&sq=
crisis%20averted%20road%20still%20slick&st=cse.

———. "Complaint Withdrawn; Skaters Are Cleared." *The New
York Times.* January 25, 2002. Available online. URL: http://
query.nytimes.com/gst/fullpage.html?res=9A07E7DB163AF9
36A15752C0A9649C8B63.

———. "Defamation Suit Filed." *The New York Times.* January 18,
2002. Available online. URL: http://query.nytimes.com/gst/
fullpage.html?res=9C04E3D91F38F93BA25752C0A9649C8
B63&scp=1&sq=olympics%20defamation%20suit%20filed&
st=cse.

———. "Fix Charge Is a Threat to Skater Ohno." *The New York
Times.* January 22, 2002. Available online. URL: http://query.
nytimes.com/gst/fullpage.html?res=9C00E6D7123BF931A1
5752C0A9649C8B63&n=Top/Reference/Times%20Topics/
People/O/Ohno,%20Apolo%20Anton&scp=1&sq=fix%20
charge%20is%20threat%20ohno&st=cse.

Rocchio, Christopher. "Apolo Anton Ohno Training Hard to
Capture Olympic and 'Dancing' Gold." *Reality TV World.*
April 26, 2007. Available online. URL: http://www.reality
tvworld.com/news/apolo-anton-ohno-training-hard-capture-
olympic-and-dancing-gold-5099.php.

"Sports Briefing: Successful Return for Ohno." *The New York
Times.* March 10, 2007. Available online. URL: http://query.
nytimes.com/gst/fullpage.html?res=9D02E4D91331F933A25
750C0A9619C8B63&scp=1&sq=speedskating%20successful
%20return%20for%20ohno&st=cse.

United Press International. "Apolo Ohno Dances Off a Winner."
UPI NewsTrack. May 22, 2007.

"Video: Apolo Anton Ohno & Julianne Hough Dish on 'Relationship.'" May 25, 2007. Available online. URL: http://www.
people.com/people/article/0,,1545936_20040384,00.html.

Wallner, Rosemary. *Japanese Immigrants: 1850–1950*. (Coming to America.) Mankato, Minn.: Blue Earth Books, 2002.

Zinser, Lynn. "Ohno Leaves Competition Behind at the Olympic Trials." *The New York Times*. December 16, 2005. Available online. URL: http://query.nytimes.com/gst/fullpage.html?res =9800E5DD1F31F937A25751C1A9639C8B63&&scp=1&sq= skating%20ohno%20kim%20hold%20lead&st=cse.

———. "Skating; Ohno (Despite Collision) and Kim Hold Lead at Short-Track Trials." *The New York Times*. December 14, 2005. Available online. URL: http://query.nytimes.com/gst/fullpage. html?res=9800E5DD1F31F937A25751C1A9639C8B63&& scp=1&sq=skating%20ohno%20kim%20hold%20lead&st =cse.

FURTHER RESOURCES

BOOKS

Judd, Ron C. *The Winter Olympics: An Insider's Guide to the Legends, Lore and Events of the Games.* (Vancouver Edition). Seattle, Wash.: The Mountaineers Books, 2008.

Publow, Barry. *Speed on Skates: A Complete Technique, Training, and Racing Guide for In-Line and Ice Skaters.* Champaign, Ill.: Human Kinetics Publishers, 1999.

U.S. Olympic Committee. (Ed.) *A Basic Guide to Speed Skating.* (Olympic Guides). Strongsville, Ohio: Gareth Stevens Publishing, 2002.

Wallechinksy, David, and Jaime Loucky. *The Complete Book of the Winter Olympics: Turin 2006 Edition.* Toronto, Canada: SportClassic Books, 2005.

Woods, Ronald B. *Social Issues in Sport.* Champaign, Ill.: Human Kinetics Publishers, 2007.

WEB SITES

Apolo Anton Ohno: The Official Site
http://www.apoloantonohno.com

International Olympic Committee
http:/ www.olympic.org

International Skating Union Official Site
http://www.isu.org

U.S. Speedskating
http://www.usspeedskating.org

PHOTO CREDITS

INDEX

ABOUT
THE AUTHOR

REBECCA ALDRIDGE has been a writer and editor for more than 13 years. In addition to this title, she has written several nonfiction children's books, including titles on Thomas Jefferson, Italian immigrants in America, the *Titanic,* and the Hoover Dam. As an editor, she has had input on more than 50 children's books covering such diverse topics as social activism, vegetarian eating, and tattooing and body piercing. She lives in Minneapolis, Minnesota.